Judicial Craftsmanship or Fiat?

CONTRIBUTIONS IN POLITICAL SCIENCE

Series Editor: **Bernard K. Johnpoll**

American Democratic Theory: Pluralism and Its Critics
William Alton Kelso

International Terrorism in the Contemporary World
Marius H. Livingston, editor

Doves and Diplomats: Foreign Offices and Peace Movements in
Europe and America in the 20th Century
Solomon Wank, editor

Believing Skeptics: American Political Intellectuals, 1945-1964
Robert Booth Fowler

Locke, Rousseau, and the Idea of Consent: An Inquiry into the
Liberal-Democratic Theory of Political Obligation
Jules Steinberg

The Capitol Press Corps: Newsmen and the Governing of New
York State
David R. Morgan

Judicial Craftsmanship or Fiat?

DIRECT OVERTURN BY THE UNITED STATES SUPREME COURT

Howard Ball

Contributions in Political Science, Number 7

GREENWOOD PRESS
WESTPORT, CONNECTICUT ● LONDON, ENGLAND

Library of Congress Cataloging in Publication Data

Ball, Howard, 1937-
     Judicial craftsmanship or fiat?
     (Contributions in political science; no. 7
ISSN 0147-1066)
     Bibliography: p.
     Includes index.
     1. United States. Supreme Court. 2. Judicial
review—United States. 3. Political questions and
judicial power—United States. I. Title. II Series.
KF8748.B24   347.73′26   77-91102
ISBN 0-313-20035-1

Library of Congress Catalog Card Number: 77-91102
ISBN: 0-313-20035-1
ISSN: 0147-1066

First published in 1978

Greenwood Press, Inc.
51 Riverside Avenue, Westport, Connecticut 06880

Printed in the United States of America

10 9 8 7 6 5 4 3 2 1

*For Carol's dad, Susan, Sheryl, and
Melissa's grandpa, and my
fishing companion: Sidney Neidell*

Contents

Acknowledgments

This book would not have been possible without the help and guidance of some very fine people at Mississippi State University. I wish to thank the Office of Research and Graduate Studies for the financial assistance that enabled me to complete the research and the first draft of the manuscript. I also want to thank Vice-President Chester McKee, Dean Lyell Behr, and Associate Deans Lewis Brown and Charles Lowery for their advice and support.

A great deal of the research was done in Montana, and I would be remiss if I did not thank the people at the University of Montana School of Law, especially Carole Ann Granger, assistant law librarian, and Mary Lou Cordis and Rosie Grey. For just being themselves, I must thank Bob and Sonja Bassett, Betty and Youngie Paaske, Bob Wolff, Jamie and Kate Edwards and their family, and the assorted brown and rainbow trout of Rock Creek in Montana. These very fine people and the fish in that magnificent creek enabled me to return to the research and the writing reinvigorated and refreshed.

I also want to thank Bernard Johnpoll, an old friend and colleague from our days at Rutgers University, for encouraging me to expand an essay I had prepared for the American Political Science Association meetings at Washington, D.C., in September 1977. A word of thanks for the support and encouragement offered by James Sabin of Greenwood Press during the early stages of the research project.

Finally I owe a great debt of gratitude to my women, for they gave me the greatest help and support and love on this project.

Carol, my lovely wife, let me work unabated even though it meant not having a husband around for a great many weeks while I was traveling to Missoula and writing and typing in the trailer. She did not complain when I went off by myself to fish and to reflect—but did have some words when I returned "skunked" for the day. My little women, Susan, Sheryl, and Melissa, allowed me to work in relative peace and quiet—even though this meant chasing them out of the house on occasion. I think they understood why I chased them. Their putting up with me meant a lot, and I want to thank my women, big and little, for giving me that time to work.

Introduction

Attending graduate school in the Kennedy era, I was impressed with the activities of the Warren Court. In the eyes of young liberal graduate students the Court was in the forefront in the battles against racial injustice and inequality. The Warren Court, the result-oriented defender of the rights of the oppressed in our society, was sacrosanct. All the critical commentaries of my professor of public law at Rutgers University, Stanley Friedelbaum, and the essays by constitutional scholars such as Herbert Wechsler, especially his "Toward Neutral Principles of Constitutional Law," in the 1959 *Harvard Law Review*, were greeted with a mixture of contempt and bafflement by my fellow students. The Court was, after all, doing good things, and to force it to adhere to "neutral principles" in constitutional adjudication would be to restrain the only national agency with the willingness to attempt to resolve these problems. How could a tribunal be neutral in the face of these societal dilemmas that needed resolution?

This book is an attempt to point out that it is necessary for the Supreme court to decide cases and controversies, especially constitutional cases, on grounds of adequate neutrality and generality. In the final analysis, with respect to the notion of rule of law and respect for judicial tribunals in our society, "the virtue or demerit of a judgment turns entirely on the reasons that support it and their adequacy to maintain any choice of values it decrees."[1] The basic difference between the Supreme Court and the popularly elected agencies of the national government is that the Court must provide sound, principled reasons when it decides a controversy properly before the justices. It is quite easy for nine men, or a majority of these nine, to reach agreement on the results, or final determination, of litigation. But for these justices to render their decision without providing adequate reasons, grounded in the Constitution, history, precedent, or events that modify past precedent, is to decide by fiat and decree.

The function of the courts, especially the Supreme Court of the United States, is to decide controversies by explanation, persuasion, and reasoned justification. Deciding cases on other grounds, or no evident grounds whatsoever by simply deciding on an ad hoc basis, has adverse consequences for the Court. Whims and caprice lead to naked conclusions that can only weaken "and impair the respect in which the Court is held and thus weaken its institutional position."[2] If the judgment of the Supreme Court is simply the personal preferences of the judges, then the Court is another partisan political actor.

Forcing fallible men who are justices of the Supreme Court to decide cases and controversies in a principled, craftsmanlike manner enables them to transcend their own value biases—or at least to buttress their values with reasons that are general and part of the jurisprudential fabric of the society. Ad hoc evaluations of the Constitution are fine for legislators, presidents, and others who must make important decisions for society in time of crisis. These ad hoc views can be examined by the courts, employing that uniquely American power of judicial review. And these courts can validate these judgments of legislators and others, or invalidate them, but the judges must do so in a manner that can withstand criticism from scholars and disobedience from political actors.

When the Supreme Court invalidates a judgment of the Congress or of the president, it must write an opinion that analyzes the legislation in light of constitutional principles and must indicate in a reasoned argument why the legislation failed to pass constitutional muster. If the Court cannot do that—even though the majority believes the legislation unwise—then the legislation ought not to be invalidated. For the Court to strike down or validate an act of Congress simply because it disagrees or agrees is to function as a "naked power organ."[3] The Court is, must be, more than that type of agency. For the opinions to have legal (as opposed to ideological) quality, they must rest on the legal foundations of reasoned argument, constitutional fidelity, precedent, and the awareness of the historical dimension.

An opinion of the Court, a reasoned principled opinion, is a work of art. It is judicial craftsmanship. It is a judgment based on adequate reasons, grounded in constitutional prerequisites, and transcends the personal idiosyncrasies of five or more men on the Court. To act constantly on this high plateau is a difficult if not impossible demand to make on fallible men. But the Supreme Court is the highest court in America, and we must make that demand. For it to act in less than a principled manner is to weaken the legal foundation in America. If the Court majority produces opinions that are fiat, then the responsibility of the scholar is to condemn that practice, regardless of the apparent goodness of the judgment.

If a hallmark of civilization is the peaceful, equitable resolution of conflict in the courtroom, then the court must constantly strive to arrive at decisions that are principled and reasoned. Decree or fiat by courts will eventually lead to failure of the legal system because losers would rightfully conclude that they lost because of the makeup of the judges and nothing more or less. We must be given something more than personal decrees for us to accept and to be obedient to the law. Decree and fiat signal the end of a civilization. When people lose respect for the integrity of the legal system, then we are left with the potential for anarchy.

When the Supreme Court concludes that an earlier opinion of that Court was erroneous and that it must be reversed, the reversal must be done in a principled manner. The object of this book is to examine the ways in which Supreme Courts have overturned their earlier opinions. The thesis posited is that when the Court overturns, it must base its stance on one of three justifications: rightness, factual correctness, and constitutional principles. When the Court majority acts in this manner, it is creating reasonable craftsmanlike opinions. When it overturns in another manner, it is acting as an ideological, result-oriented group of legislators.

The justices' fidelity is to the law, not to partisan interests. A partisan Supreme Court is a fundamental danger to the stability of our society. If there is evidence of lack of craftsmanship in the legal art of judicial overturn, then a warning signal must be struck. A constitutional system cannot long endure if the judges themselves do not honor its basic precepts. Civilization falls to the extent that the law and the judges fail to act in a principled manner. We must expect our judges to act equitably and in a principled manner, especially when they overturn earlier Court judgments. Anything less is sloppy justice, and our legal system cannot long endure in the face of ideological decisions from the nation's highest tribunal.

NOTES

1. Herbert Wechsler, "Toward Neutral Principles in Constitutional Law," *Harvard Law Review* 73 (1959):20.

2. David Curries, "The Supreme Court and Federal Jurisdiction: 1975 Term," *1976 The Supreme Court Review* (Chicago: University of Chicago Press, 1977), p. 218.

3. Wechsler, *op. cit.*, p. 19.

Judicial Craftsmanship or Fiat?

1 Law, Stare Decisis, and Social Change

LAW AND SOCIAL CHANGE

At some early stage in its development, a social community will agree on a set of values dealing with its fundamental public problems and issues "on which the existence of that society depends."[1] This agreed-upon set of values is the essence of law, for law in society makes certain kinds of conduct obligatory through stated norms; it consists of a body of rules, principles, and standards of conduct that are binding in the community.[2] The legal order also determines the methods by which the law is created, declared, enforced, and changed; it is backed by mechanisms that ensure societal compliance with its rules.[3]

Law is the body of statutes, principles, standards of social conduct, and rules made by the governors that must be obeyed by all who live in the community. Law in America, wrote Roscoe Pound, consists of *legal precepts* (the common law) structured by courts, legislators, bureaucrats, and executives (statutory law, administrative law, executive orders, and judge-made law) *techniques or rules* for obeying, modifying, or changing the law (steps for amending the Constitution, repealing legislation, judicial review by the courts, stare decisis), and the *"ideal element"* or authoritative ideals of the community (the U.S. Constitution and the principles it contains).[4]

The last element in Pound's classification scheme of law in America emphasizes "an ideal picture of the society we are living in and things that accord with what are reasonable. It is authoritative, it is traditional, it is handed down and governs, or ought to govern, just as much as the legal precept itself."[5] Such principles as justice, equality, domestic tranquility, and liberty found in the Constitution are the lodestars for the community, the ideals we aspire to. They ought to be the basis for the statutes, rules, judicial decisions pronounced by the rule makers. Theoretically the rule makers of the society are continually trying to operationalize these ideals.

In sum, the three sources of law in America are constitutional law, statutory and administrative law, and the common law (or judge-made law). The last two are made in light of the Constitution and the parameters of power it gives to legislators, executives, and judges. The Constitution is the fundamental law for America, it is not just a text, it is a tradition.[6] These three sources of law bind the American community and give the members of the community a sense of place, a feeling of stability and certitude, a sense of knowing that the rights, privileges, and duties they had yesterday are theirs today and probably tomorrow, and a sense of knowing what to expect in their day-to-day social, economic, and business relationships with others in the community. These sources of law allow people to function without undue alarm about the character of their relationships with their family, friends, peers, business associates, enemies, institutions, and politicians. In short, the law provides Americans with security. (Theodore White's book on Nixon and Watergate is titled *Breach of Faith*; his point is that Richard Nixon's actions as president violated the trust and faith Americans placed and had in the chief executive. Americans felt secure in the knowledge that their political leader—the president—was acting in a manner consistent with the constitutional requisites; Nixon's crime was to violate the trust Americans had developed toward the office).[7]

Consistent with the ideal element of law, the public desires fairness, uniformity, and impartiality as well as stability: "Law should be reasonably consistent and coherent and have as one of its prime characteristics a reasonable predictability."[8] We identify the law with logic: "Stability is the child of logic, of clear and definite standards and of the absence of conflict."[9] We wish—and act out our lives with the expectation that the wish is reality—to find in the law formal and symmetrical structures of logical propositions "all neatly dovetailed. Truth or error . . . would be determined by checking to see whether it fitted into a symmetrical structure."[10]

As Supreme Court Justice Oliver W. Holmes said, the law will become entirely consistent only when it ceases to grow.[11] While the law does act as a stabilizing force in the community, it is also an instrument of social change:

> Under a facade of formal symmetry it must honor reasonable expectations born of the past, yet allow *lebensraum* for the present and the future. Law is constantly adopting new principles from current needs at one end and gradually sloughing off old ones at the other. . . . Law is not a bucket of ready-made answers, but a reconciling process. Its role is to channel conflicting social energies into peaceful accommodations—the endless sequence of accommodations that we call civilization.[12]

In the law of an ongoing, nonstagnant society (or non-Platonic republics ruled by non-philosopher-kings), there is always a basic tension between the "principled universe of logic and the expedient requirements of experience."[13] This essential contradiction in law mirrors the human condition.

The interests in society served by the symmetry and certainty of the law must constantly be balanced against the social interests served by equity, fairness, justice, and other elements of social welfare. In the American and other democratic societies, this is the fundamental struggle between the haves and the have nots, between the ins and the outs, between the people on top of the hill and others struggling to get up. For those on the top, the law's stability is all important. Law helped them get to that plateau; the stability of law will keep them there. For the people who are still struggling, the law needs to be modified in order for them to achieve the good life.

Inequities that arise from the existence of laws in society— slavery, industrial evils and unfair treatment of labor, racial discrimination—must be dealt with fairly if the society is to continue to function and grow.[14] If the law is responsible for these evils, it also plays a significant part in the resolution or amelioration of these dilemmas. The law changes as society changes—except for the ideal element, the Constitution, unless formally amended. (Although the Constitution is interpreted anew constantly by legislators, judges, and executives, it is interpreted with an eye constantly on the basic principles contained in it.)

The history of law is a history of growth in America. The issue is one of pace, change, tempo.[15] In a democracy, changes in the law reflect a change in the thinking of the people. Law, to paraphrase Holmes, is a flow of events and reflects this flow of events; it is not a static system.[16] If the law is a "product of present hopes and past traditions"[17]; if law is "forever adopting new principles from life at one end and it always retains old ones from history at the other"[18]; if law "undergoes constant change, every period is transitional, tying what went before to what is to come after"[19]; and if there is a psychic need for continuity and stability in the law, then there must be a balance struck between adherence to the logic, and stability, of the past law and adjustment and change in present-day law. Constant changes in the system of law, even the appearance of constant change, can damage the community irreparably. If standards of human conduct—in business, politics, social life—lose their illusion of certainty, then the fabric that binds society may very well disintegrate.

"Certainty and change are the great antinomies of the law," wrote Justice Benjamin Cardozo.[20] If the law must change with changing social conditions, and it must, then change must flow from the enduring principles, the ideal element, that binds the community. The Constitution is "more like a tree, striking its roots deep into the soil of human experience, sending up fresh shoots and putting out new limbs to meet the needs of an ever-expanding civilization. It has continuity, life, growth."[21]

Continuity and change occur when the rule makers remember that their actions in forging new law and replacing old must accord with the timeless principles of the fundamental law: the Constitution. Supreme Court Justice Benjamin Cardozo wrote that the progress of the law is shaped by certain basic forces: logic, history, custom, utility, and "accepted standards of right conduct."[22] These standards of right conduct are found in the Constitution and in its interstices. The rule of law exists when legislators, judges, and executives develop legal precepts in reasonable accordance with the fundamental law of the land. So long as the policymakers act in this reasonable, statesmanlike manner will there be equilibrium between the forces calling for change and the demand for stability and continuity.

COURTS AND CHANGES IN THE LAW

The dynamics of change and stability occur in Congress and the White House and produce new public laws, revisions in statutes, and so forth; but the focus of this volume is on the way in which courts, especially the United States Supreme Court, have dealt with the issue of stability and change in the common law and in the law of the Constitution itself.

Traditionally courts in America have functioned as the resolvers of the conflict between the forces of stability and those that have demanded changes in society by challenging the laws of the land. "We Americans legalize our politics," said Henry Abraham. "Sooner or later in America every political question inexorably becomes a legal question."[23] Judges, wrote Chief Justice Earl Warren in 1955, "are not monks or scientists, but participants in the living stream of our national life, steering the law between the dangers of rigidity on the one hand and formlessness on the other."[24]

Judicial changing of the law, and the costs involved with respect to the need for stability, is the focus of this study. Using the techniques of litigation—standing to sue, ripeness, personal injury, stare decisis, non-hohfeldian plaintiff argumentation, and so forth —claimants come to the courts challenging the existing law and/or the manner of its application in their case. Judges, employing the power of judicial review, have constantly attempted to maintain that crucial tension between change and certainty in the law by carefully examining the arguments of the litigants who come before them.[25] They ask the judges to seek solutions to "difficult and delicate problems of public concern."[26] The judges respond to these arguments in the light of their understanding of the fundamental law of the Constitution and should adjudicate in the light of these enduring values.

All courts possess this power of judicial review, this "principled process of enunciating and applying endless values of our society" when deciding cases and controversies that come to them.[27] With this judicial activity comes change in the law. As Dean Roscoe Pound noted, "Law must be stable, yet it cannot stand still."[28] In this difficult task of determining which interest outweights another, "judicial labor at its highest level,"[29] the judge must get his knowledge "just as the the legislator gets his, from experience, and study and reflection; in brief, from life itself."[30]

Judges must steer their way between change and continuity in order to arrive at the just, equitable, and reasonable decision in the case before them. In arriving at what is to them the just decision, they draw from life experiences and from their profession: "the heritage of the law, the spirit of Anglo-Saxon law, the impact of cases—in short, the taught tradition of the law."[31] *Stare decisis et non quieta movere*—"stand by the precedents and do not disturb the calm"—is a basic ingredient in that taught tradition of law in America.

STARE DECISIS

Scholars maintain that stare decisis, adherence to precedent, "arose from a desire for certainty and continuity in the law."[32] Some argue that "it is a principle inherent in every legal system . . .for the earliest form of law is custom and the core of custom is precedent."[33] Stare decisis, a deductive process whereby judges draw upon general principles of law contained in earlier decisions to decide cases, is intimately associated with Anglo-Saxon law. In English law, precedent means that a final judicial pronouncement on a legal question has been made, and stare decisis arises only when cases are presented that raise the identical point of law.

The finding of similarity by the judge between the present situation and points of law developed in past cases is the heart of the process of stare decisis. Blackstone, the noted eighteenth-century English legal commentator, wrote that, with respect to the doctrine of stare decisis, "judges should be sworn to determine not according to his own private judgment but according to the known laws and customs of the land; not delegated to pronounce a new law but to maintain and expound the old one."[34] The precedent controlling the judgment is found by the judge's taking into account what he considers to be material facts and by disregarding immaterial ones.[35] Stare decisis suggests that judges adhere to settled points of law when deciding cases and controversies.

Stare decisis doctrine has been referred to as the three Cs: "(1) *clarity;* we must know what the law is, (2) *consistency;* equality of treatment under the law, and (3) *certainty;* avoid the introduction of doubt into the law through judicial departures of precedent."[36] Americans inherited from England this tradition of courts' deciding cases in light of historically developed general principles and, "instead of merely giving judgment, the court must explain in a reasoned opinion why A must pay B."[37] It has become a "basic postulate of American case law" that the judgment of a court majority, and only a court majority that agrees on the ruling and not the final result, establishes a precedent for use by that court and others in subsequent adjudications.[38]

Stare decisis, said Associate Justice William O. Douglas, Jr., of the United States Supreme Court, "provides some moorings so that men may trade and arrange their affairs with confidence. It serves to take the capricious element out of the law and to give stability to a society. It is a strong tie which the future has to the past."[39] Given the existence of the doctrine, the societal assumption is that cases will be disposed of fairly and impartially—mechanically— by the judicial application of known principles of law. Without this assumption, "our common law [judge-made law] process would become the most intolerable kind of *ex post facto* judicial law making."[40] As another Supreme Court justice, Felix Frankfurter, expressed it: "We do not sit like Kadi under a tree, dispensing justice according to considerations of individual expediency."[41]

Arthur J. Goldberg, former associate justice of the United States Supreme Court, suggested that there were at least five practical reasons for the doctrine of stare decisis: (1) it fosters public confidence in judicial decision making by giving the appearance of impersonal, consistent, and reasoned opinions; (2) respect for the doctrine induces a greater impersonality of decision and buttresses judges against their own natural tendencies and prejudices; (3) it facilitates private ordering; (4) it eases the judicial burden by discouraging suits; and (5) justice in the instant case is served by eliminating the injustices of unfair surprise and unequal treatment.[42] In sum precedent generally "governs the conclusions and surrounds the reasoning of lawyers and judges."[43] The lawyer has the highest chance of winning if he or she can show a court that the client must win "if the court keeps doing exactly what it has been doing," the next best chance of winning if he or she can "persuade the court that it should do exactly what some other court has been doing," the next best chance of winning if he or she can convince the judge "to do something slightly different from what he or some other court has been doing," and the worst chance of winning "if he [or she] must argue that the Court should do something markedly different from what it and other courts have done in the past."[44]

The basic social interest of stare decisis is fairness of treatment through uniformity and impartiality. As justice is the goal and the "doing" of justice the function of courts, "in the main there shall be adherence to precedent." However, "uniformity ceases to be a good when it becomes uniformity of oppression."[45] In the interest of societal certainty and stability in adjudication, courts will adhere to precedent until doing so leads to perpetuation of injustice and inequity. While the law has its rules, statutes, and precedents, "through the observance of which we may extricate ourselves from many predicaments," the law does change.

If we cling too closely to precedent, we may perpetuate error. Under a changeless law we must stagnate, however sound the rule may have been at its birth. If we disregard precedent, we lose the value of the law as a stabilizer of human affairs. Stare decisis maintains the balance.[46]

This attitude is paradigmatic of the realist school of jurisprudence. For the realist, stare decisis is a useful tool in the taught tradition of the law, but it "is not an inexorable command."[47] Associate Justice Benjamin Cardozo summed up the realist position on stare decisis:

If we figure stability and progress as opposite poles, then at one pole we have the maxim of *stare decisis* and the method of decision by the tool of a deductive logic; at the other we have the method which subordinates means to ends. Each method has its value, and for each in the changes of litigation there will come an hour for use. A wise eclecticism employs them both.[48]

The legal realist therefore realized that precedent and stare decisis are important elements of American law, but they have certain limitations.[49]

In addition to the changing attitude toward the traditional concept of case law "as a process of neutral decision making through the rational application of case precedent, established principle, and sound policy,"[50] another equally potent impact on the doctrine of stare decisis has been the recent proliferation of legal cases and materials in American law.[51] From 1776 to the turn of the twentieth century, the digests of all reported cases in the state and federal court systems fill three shelves in a law library. In the following sixty-year period, 1900-1960, the digests of the reported opinions fill over thirty shelves in that law library.[52]

With all these potential sources for the legal community to draw upon, there are "plenty of precedents to go around; and with the accumulation of decisions it is no great problem for the lawyer to find legal authority for most propositions."[53] This increase in the number of judicial opinions and, consequently, precedents has the "effect of deprecating the value of precedent."[54] When there are too many cases and precedents, that mass, "indifferently decided, precludes the winnowing of the good decisions from the mass of case law by doctrines of precedent alone."[55] When the lawyer has dozens of cases to cite as controlling precedent today, rather than the two or three citations that used to be the case in litigation a short while ago, with many of the cases nearly identical on their facts, but "decided every which way," what is a court or a judge to do?[56] The answer, suggested some time ago by the legal realists, is that the judge uses reasoned judgment in selecting the precedent that he or she believes is correct in the context of that particular litigation.

STARE DECISIS AS A RULE OF POLICY

American judges have been taught to exercise judgment in suits in light of the necessity of maintaining stability and uniformity in the case law; the doctrine of stare decisis is more than a mere mechanical formula that can be operationalized by computer technicians. Reflecting the limitations enumerated above, for many scholars the reality of the doctrine of stare decisis is that it is a "principle of policy and not a mechanical formula."[57]

There is no "antithesis between precedent and policy; they are complementary."[58] Each precedent or general principle of law reflects a particular social policy. The judge has to make the choice of what prior principle or rule will be used in deciding the controversy before the court. Whether a precedent will be followed, modified, ignored, or overturned "depends on whether the policies which underlie the proposed rule [suggested by lawyers in the instant litigation] are strong enough to outweigh both the policies which support the existing rule and the disadvantages of making the change."[59]

Confronting a balancing situation, the judge weighs the impact of past precedent/policy against the fact that the law must grow and change with the times—although it must do so incrementally. In this evaluatory dilemma, the wise jurist, said Justice Cardozo, is the eclectic jurist; he is the judge who understands that the doctrine of stare decisis has two elements, the dynamic and the static. The first element is judicial acknowledgment that the law must progress; the second "reminds us that stability and certainty, rather than growth and change, are often higher values."[60] The wise judge, the statesman-jurist, seeks to blend the two elements by taking into account when judging, "in due proportion," the general wisdom of the past and the needs of the present.[61] Stare decisis cannot stand in the way of progress; neither can it be ignored without damaging the continuity of law in America. Stare decisis as a fundamental social policy is just this tension between continuity and change. Courts and judges in America have to grapple with this existential legal reality continuously and, said one associate justice of the Supreme Court, Potter Stewart, ruefully, "Wisdom too often never comes."[62]

This judicial statesmanship requires principled adjudication. In the weighing of competing demands for stability and change, judges must return to the general principles of the law, embodied in the Constitution, to reach a reasoned judgment in the case before them.[63]

STARE DECISIS AND THE CONSTITUTION

When a court in America confronts litigation involving the Constitution itself, it is confronting a legal problem of the first magnitude. The 1787 Constitution is the ideal element of American law, the highest law, the supreme law of the land. Constitutional questions deal with the nature of governmental power and its limits. Unlike other kinds of law, constitutional law "is more a matter of government than rule-making."[64] Radiating from that document are the powers of government—state and national—by and through which all other rules, statutes, and policies are created. Therefore, when it hears a constitutional issue and examines precedents involving the meaning of a constitutional clause, a court arrives at the very center of its stare decisis existential dilemna.

"We must never forget that it is a Constitution we are expounding," wrote Chief Justice John Marshall in *McCulloch* v *Maryland,* an 1819 decision of the Supreme Court. It is "a constitution intended to endure for ages to come and, consequently, to be adapted to the various crises of human affairs."[65] Stare decisis, according to Marshall's statement, is the "gloss which [a judge's predecessors] may have put on [the Constitution]."[66] If it is the words of the Constitution itself that the judges must expound and not the patina and gloss and definitions and "excrescences" given to its phrases by earlier court majorities, then the place of stare decisis in constitutional law litigation can be described as tenuous.[67] "Where the public interest and general welfare are involved, it is more important that the law be settled right than it merely be settled."[68] Courts involved in litigation involving the meaning of the Constitution must constantly test their conclusions by the Constitution itself, the "organic document," rather than by following precedent alone.[69]

Some argue that the Constitution has survived for almost two centuries because of its adaptability (through judicial reexamination of the meaning of its phrases) to deal with problems faced by succeeding generations of Americans. "Through a process of updating the document itself (by returning to various interpretations of the Constitutions by earlier court majorities or by expounding on the meaning of the Constitution itself), the Supreme Court has acted as a continuing constitutional convention."[70] The lifeblood of America's "living constitution" are the authoritative ideals, the enduring political and social principles themselves.[71] A viable adaption of the law of the Constitution to new social demands "requires the guiding force of political principle.[72] And this adaption requires judicial statesmanship of the highest order.

Judicial statesmanship is the ability of a court to adapt the Constitution in a principled, purposive manner; "the ability to rationalize a constitutional judgement in terms of principles referable to accepted sources of law is an essential major element of constitutional adjudication."[73] The art of judicial statesmanship consists of weaving principles and facts into "a judicial fabric strong and resilient enough to withstand the wear and tear of modern society while remaining faithful to a design established long ago."[74] Without this judicial linking of enduring principle to present-day adjudication, "we might well approach a ruleless, principleless situation in our constitutional law."[75]

A judge, when examining arguments and deciding cases that raise constitutional issues, must necessarily restrain himself when he grapples with the controversy. A primary restraint is his understanding that "it is a Constitution which he swore to support and defend" and not his perceptions of what the document should have said.[76] Judges and their opinions always remain inferior to the basic document itself.

THE MODIFICATION OF PRECEDENT

There are occasions when the judge, or court majority, believes that earlier court interpretations of the Constitution were inconsistent with the enduring ideal elements of that document or have led to the development of societal inequity and injustice because of consequences unforeseen by the original court majority.[77]

These factors may, in the words of Justice Cardozo, "enjoin upon the judge the duty of drawing the line at another angle, of staking the path along new courses, of marking a new point of departure from which others who come after him will set out upon their journey."[78] Judges doing justice will react to these dilemmas in their own way, influenced by the taught traditions of the law and their own life experiences. They will apply precedent when it is reasonable to do so; they should draw lines at other angles and generally "extend those precedents creatively" to situations where the facts and changing events do not fit the precedent mold.[79]

Judicial creativeness, the drawing of angles and the staking of new paths for others to follow, paralleling the concept of judicial statesmanship, is the "extension of legal categories and perhaps the creation of new categories of judicial relevance" in light of the enduring political and social principles within the Constitution. [80] Judges and court majorities change the case law within the taught traditions of the law by creatively distinguishing, limiting, or ignoring earlier precedents.

Limiting precedent occurs when a court narrows the scope of an earlier opinion without directly overturning it. The Supreme Court "rarely overturns decisions in explicit terms, preferring instead to squeeze the life from them" by the narrowing process.[81] Distinguishing precedent occurs when a court majority finds the fact-law situation sufficiently dissimilar from that of an earlier opinion. The earlier opinion, not narrowed, still retains its full scope but has been found to be "not controlling" or not applicable to the case or controversy at hand. Ignoring precedent, somewhat more disingenuous than the other judicial strategies, occurs when the court majority elects to ignore one line of (allegedly) relevant precedent for another.[82]

Acting in this oftentimes creative manner, judges and court majorities can and do change the case law while retaining the genial fiction of adhering to the doctrine of stare decisis. There is change with continuity, for the court majority modifies the common law while at the same time preserving the notion that they are disinterested judges mechanically finding and applying fixed rules of the common law. "Such back-handed emasculation of precedent" is a necessary court tool that has to balance the needs of the present and future with the traditions and certainty of the past.[83]

There have been times, however, where judicial creativeness and statesmanship have forced the court majority to overturn its earlier opinions because the tactics of distinguishing, limiting, and ignoring do not work. The United States Supreme Court, since its inception, has had to overturn earlier Court decisions a hundred times.[84]

SUMMARY

Societies create legal order, reflecting customs and traditions and ideals, in order to grow and mature. The legal system of a society contains the fundamental principles by which the society is organized and provides for the peaceful resolution of controversy by developing standards of public conduct, obligatory for all, that stress fairness, uniformity, impartiality, and psychic certainty. In American society, the hallmark of law is the concept of equal justice under law.

The law must change to meet the growing needs of the society. The great antinomies of the law are certainty and change, and a balance must be struck between the two forces. Change must come but it must be consistent with the enduring principles of the fundamental law in America, the Constitution of 1787. This is the essence of judicial statesmanship, judicial labor at its highest: judges must be eclectic, weighing the competing demands of change and certainty in light of the timeless principles of the Constitution and render judgment accordingly.

Stare decisis is an important aspect of the legal order. Calling for adherence to prior decisions of a court, the doctrine reflects certainty and stability of law. But it too is flexible; it creates the illusion of certainty for public consumption while constantly undergoing change in light of the enduring societal principles. "We recognize that stare decisis embodies an important social policy" [stability]," wrote Justice Felix Frankfurter of the Supreme Court. "It represents an element of continuity in law, and is rooted in the psychological need to satisfy reasonable expectations."[85] Taking care not to disturb the fiction of stare decisis, judges modify precedent in light of the felt necessities of the times. Especially with respect to the law of the Constitution do the justices of the Supreme Court liberally employ the doctrine of stare decisis.

The constitutional language must be expounded by the Supreme Court in cases and controversies before the justices, not the patina

and gloss put on the phrases in that document by earlier court majorities—unless the earlier majority view is seen as binding in light
of changes in society. While stare decisis provides moorings for
people to guide their lives in security, it is not an inexorable command to the justices of the Supreme Court in constitutional cases.
So long as the members of the Supreme Court resolve controversies
that come before it in light of enduring principles and with the
knowledge that the society needs stability or the fiction of stability
and certainty, the Court acts reasonably and consistent with the
idea of rule of law.

Ignoring the dilemma of continuity and change in law and ignoring the importance of acting in light of enduring principles of the
Constitution, a court majority's decision, result oriented, lacks
linkage with the past and has the potential of disrupting the fabric
of societal stability as well as damaging the reputation of the Court.
A result-oriented Court majority, without roots in the past, can
seriously affect the nature of law in society if it continues to function in such a ruleless, principleless fashion.

The balance must continually be struck between the forces of
change and the forces of continuity. It is a difficult task for the
Supreme Court justices; they are fallible and lack knowledge of the
ultimate impact of their judgments and the correctness of their
perceptions of the meaning of the Constitution. Modification of
court decisions takes place because of the fallibility of judges; there
is no violation of the concept of law when such modification does
take place. But it must be in line with the constitutional principles
or else it is nothing less than judicial fiat.

NOTES

1. George W. Paton, *A Textbook of Jurisprudence*, 3d ed. (London:
Oxford at the Clarendon Press, 1961), p. 92.

2. H. L. A. Hart, *The Concept of Law* (London: Clarendon Press,
1961), pp. 8-31.

3. Paton, op. cit., p. 93.

4. Roscoe Pound, in Symposium, "The Status of the Rule of Judicial
Precedent," *University of Cincinnati Law Review* 14 (March 1940): 334.
"Law is not a mere collection of detailed rules, but an organic body of prin-

ciples with an inherent power of growth and adaption to new circumstances"; Paton, op. cit., p. 170.

5. Pound, op. cit.

6. Lionel Frankel, "Humanist Law: The Need for Change in Legal Education—or—If judges Do Not Find the Law, but Make It, What Do They Make It From?" *Utah Law Review*, no. 1 January 1976: 40.

7. Theodore White, *Breach of Faith: The Fall of Richard Nixon* (New York: Atheneum, 1975).

8. Herbert E. Ritchie, in Symposium, p. 261.

9. Jan G. Deutsch, "Neutrality, Legitimacy, and the Supreme Court: Some Intersections between Law and Political Science," *Stanford Law Review* 20 (1968): 235.

10. Grant Gilmore, "Legal Realism: Its Causes and Its Cure," *Yale Law Journal* 70 (June 1961): 1038.

11. Arthur J. Goldberg, *Equal Justice: The Warren Court Era of the Supreme Court* (New York: Farrar, Straus, and Giroux, 1971), p. 79, quoting Justice Holmes.

12. Wallace Mendelson, "Law and the Development of Nations," *Journal of Politics*, 32 (May 1970): 234.

13. Deutsch, op. cit., p. 236.

14. Benjamin Cardozo, *The Nature of the Judicial Process* (New Haven: Yale University Press, 1921), p. 112. "It is when the effect of a law causes a social disruption as evidenced by serious controversy in regard to fundamental change that reexamination of the tools of law need occur. Courts are dependent in this way on the social action which brings an issue into controversy since they cannot adopt a cautious stance for every minute outcry against the status quo." David Dittfurth, "Judicial Reasoning and Social Change," *Indiana Law Journal* 50 (Winter 1975): 282.

15. E. M. Wise, "The Doctrine of Stare Decisis," *Wayne State Law Review*, 21 (July 1975): 1056.

16. Arthur S. Miller, "Notes on the Concept of the 'Living' Constitution," *George Washington Law Review*, 31 (June 1963): 917.

17. Frankel, op. cit., p. 40.

18. Walter Treanor, in Symposium, p. 222.

19. Stanley Reed, "Stare Decisis and Constitutional Law," *Pennsylvania Bar Association Quarterly* 33 (October 1937): 132.

20. Miller, op. cit., p. 883, quoting Justice Cardozo.

21. Reed, op. cit., p. 132.

22. Cardozo, op. cit., p. 113.

23. Henry J. Abraham, *The Judiciary: The Supreme Court in the Governmental Process*, 4th ed., (Boston: Allyn and Bacon, 1977), p. 1.

24. Earl Warren, "The Law and the Future," *Fortune* 52 (November 1955): 106.

25. See *Marbury* v. *Madison*, 1 *Cranch* 137, 1803.

26. Abraham, op. cit., p. 161.

27. Alexander Bickel, *The Least Dangerous Branch* (Indianapolis:Bobbs-Merrill, 1962), p. 58.

28. Henry Abraham, *The Judicial Process* (New York: Oxford University Press, 1975), p. 329.

29. Albert Blaustein and Andrew Field, " 'Overruling' Opinions in the Supreme Court," *Michigan Law Review* 57 (December 1958): 166.

30. Cardozo, op. cit., p. 113.

31. Abraham, *Judicial Process*, p. 328.

32. Jon D. Noland, "Stare Decisis and the Overruling of Constitutional Decisions in the Warren Years," *Valparaiso University Law Review* 4 (June 1970): 102. See also Reed, op. cit., p. 132.

33. C. Sumner Lobingier, "Precedent in Past and Present Legal Systems," *Michigan Law Review*, 44 (September 1946): 955-56. He names, for example, the Chinese, Sumerian, Semetic, Hellenic, Roman, Romanesque, and Anglican-American civilizations as examples of societies who employed a form of stare decisis.

34. Quoted in Arthur S. Miller and D. S. Sastri, "Secrecy and the Supreme Court," *Buffalo Law Review* 22 (Spring 1973): 802.

35. See, generally, Edward Levi, *Introduction to Legal Reasoning* (Chicago: University of Chicago Press, 1960): Arthur Goodhart, "Determining the Ratio Decidendi of a Case," *Yale Law Journal* 40 (1930): 161. "The task of a court in constitutional cases is to apply a system of known rules or principles to the facts of the particular case, choosing the rule or principle relevant and applicable from among the corpus of such rules and principles available to them." Miller and Sastri, op. cit., 898.

36. Samuel Freedman, "Continuity and Change: A Task of Reconciliation," *University of British Columbia Law Review* 8 (September 1973): 209-210.

37. Gilmore, op. cit., p. 1040.

38. "Supreme Court No Clear Majority Decisions: A Study in Stare Decisis," *University of Chicago Law Review* 24 (Autumn 1956): 99; see also Lobingier, op. cit., p. 966.

39. William O. Douglas, "Stare Decisis," *Columbia Law Review* 49 (June 1949): 736.

40. Robert H. Jackson, "Decisional Law and Stare Decisis," *American Bar Association Journal* 30 (March 1944): 334: "Few would deny that stare decisis is essential to judicial decision making, Without attention to prece-

dents and the effort to make legal decisions consistent, judicial decisions would be based on the immediate results of a decision and on the moral and political commitments of a judge." William Blackstone, "Justice and Legal Reasoning," *William and Mary Law Review* 18 (Winter 1976): 322.

41. *Terminiello* v. *Chicago*, 347 U.S. 1 (1949); Cardozo wrote that while the judge has freedom to fill the "open spaces in the law," he is "not to innovate at pleasure. He is not a knight-errant roaming at will in pursuit of his own ideal of beauty or of goodness." Cardozo, op. cit., p. 141.

42. Goldberg, op. cit., pp. 75-76.

43. Charlotte Bernhardt, "Supreme Court Reversals on Constitutional Issues," *Cornell Law Quarterly* 34 (1948): 69.

44. Martin Shapiro, "Toward a Theory of Stare Decisis," *Journal of Legal Studies*, 1 (January 1972): 131.

45. Cardozo, op. cit., p. 112.

46. Reed, op. cit., p. 133.

47. Wendell Brown, "Construing the Constitution: A Trial Lawyer's Plea for Stare Decisis," *American Bar Association Journal* 44 (August 1958): 743.

48. Benjamin Cardozo, *The Paradoxes of Legal Science* (New Haven: Yale University Press, 1928), p. 8.

49. Lobingier, op. cit., pp. 973-74.

50. Frankel, op. cit., p. 39.

51. Ibid.

52. Gilmore, op. cit., p. 1041.

53. Douglas, op. cit., p. 736.

54. Fred Catlett, "The Development of the Doctrine of Stare Decisis and the Extent to Which It Should Be Applied," *Washington Law Review* 21 (1946): 169. See also Frankel, op. cit., p. 43, and Gilmore, op. cit., p. 1042.

55. Frankel, op. cit., p. 43.

56. Gilmore, op. cit., p. 1042.

57. *Helvering* v. *Hallock*, 309 U.S. 106 (1940), at 110. See also Leon Sachs, "Stare Decisis and the Legal Tender Cases," *Virginia Law Review* 20 (1934): 857, and Walter V. Shaefer, "Precedent and Policy," *University of Chicago Law Review*, 34 (1966): 24.

58. Shaefer, op. cit., p. 6.

59. Ibid.

60. Noland, op. cit., p. 103.

61. Shaefer, op. cit., p. 24.

62. *Boys Market* v. *Retail Clerks Union*, 398 U.S. 235 (1970): 355.

63. See, generally, Herbert Wechsler, "Foreword: Toward Neutral Principles in Constitutional Adjudication," *Harvard Law Review* 73 (September 1961).

64. Reed, op. cit., p. 142.

65. *McCulloch* v. *Maryland,* 17 U.S. 316, (1819): 407, 415.

66. Douglas, op. cit., p. 736.

67. Ibid.

68. Berhardt, op. cit., p. 68.

69. Reed, op. cit., p. 134.

70. Noland, op. cit., p. 131.

71. Gary Jacobsohn, "Constitutional Adjudication and Judicial Statesmanship," *Emory Law Journal* 23 (Winter 1974): 140.

72. Ibid., p. 137.

73. Goldberg, op. cit., p. 73, quoting Archibald Cox.

74. Jacobsohn, op. cit., p. 150.

75. Reed, op. cit., p. 134; Blackstone, op. cit., pp. 322-323.

76. Douglas, op. cit., p. 737.

77. See, generally, Ball, *The Warren Court's Perceptions of Democracy,* (Rutherford, N.J.: Fairleigh Dickinson University Press, 1971).

78. Cardozo, *Nature,* p. 114.

79. Blackstone, op. cit., p. 323.

80. Ibid., p. 326.

81. "Lower Court Disavowal of Supreme Court Precedent," *Virginia Law Review* 60 (1974): 511.

82. Walter Murphy and C. Herman Pritchett, editors, *Courts, Judges, and Politics* (New York: Random House, 1975), pp. 380ff.

83. "Lower Court Disavowal," p. 514.

84. Blaustein and Field, op. cit., p. 153.

85. Felix Frankfurter, *Helvering* v. *Hallock,* 309 U.S. 106 (1940).

2 Direct Overturn of Precedent and Judicial Statesmanship

The interaction of judicial decisions, precedent, principles, and the justices' views regarding the taught traditions of the law in America rules out certainty as a realistic view of the judicial process. Although some of the problems that come before the courts can be decided in one way, and the judge "in these situations must plunge the knife with averted gaze' " the major constitutional cases that come before the Supreme Court are fraught with conflict: conflicting interpretations of the facts in the case; conflicting precedents presented to the justices; conflicting interpetations of the principles involved; and differences with respect to priorities among these principles presented in the briefs and in oral argument.[1] Because of this essential uncertainty, "the judge must live with it and must decide in which direction the balance seems to point."[2]

Because of the uncertainty, yet with the necessity of maintaining the genial fiction of stability, the judicial balancing act is, or should be, a creative, statesmanlike effort. Limiting, distinguishing, and ignoring precedent are all part of this effort to balance continuity with change. Sometimes the Supreme Court must make a decision to overturn one of its earlier decisions, now precedent: "Overruling decisions represent the single group of cases that can be objectively identified as deliberate judicial vehicles of change. . . . They represent the most important unambiguous manifestation of change."[3] This traumatic change, direct overrule of earlier precedent, "represents a source of danger to both professional and popular acceptance of the Supreme Court as disinterested interpreter of the Constitution."[4] In determining when or whether to overturn, judicial statesmanship calls for a balance to be stuck between the values that inhere in consistency and the values that would "flow from the changing nature and patterns of society."[5] Justices who overturn earlier precedents must justify their decision in favor of change over continuity in a reasoned, principled manner.

DIRECT OVERTURN: SOME BASIC JUSTIFICATIONS

In justifying their decision to break sharply with precedent by overturning a decision, the justices of the Supreme Court can give three basic reasons: prior error, clarity, and/or justice.

PRIOR ERROR

Justices are human. "What is wise is not always discernible," wrote Justice Douglas.[6] "Wisdom too often never comes," wrote Justice Stewart, "and so one ought not to reject it merely because it comes late."[7] Prior judicial error has to be corrected by the justices of the Supreme Court because of the difficulty of amending the Constitution.[8] The Supreme Court should not upset precedent unless a court majority "knows with a deep and legally authenticated conviction that the prior decision or decisions of the Supreme Court were wrongly decided. Prior error must then be revealed in a declaration of law."[9]

There is an additional factor present in this justification for direct overturn: inability of other agencies to rectify prior judicial error. Justice Louis Brandeis wrote in 1932:

. . . stare decisis is usually the wise policy because in most matters it is more important that the appropriate case be settled than it be settled right. . . . In cases involving the Federal Constitution, where error correction by [congressional] action is practically impossible, this Court has often overruled its earlier opinions.[10]

Associate Justice Lewis Powell wrote the following in a 1974 opinion for the Court majority:

All prior cases lead to reconsideration, especially in matters of constitutional interpretation. It is not only our prerogative but also our duty to reexamine a precedent where its reasoning or understanding of the Constitution is fairly called into question. And if the precedent or its rationale is of doubtful validity, then it should not stand.[11]

CLARITY

If it is important that the Supreme Court be right rather than consistent, especially in regard to the meaning of the Constitution itself, some insist that it "is far more important that the law be definite than that outmoded and discredited doctrine be permitted to survive."[12] They maintain that the only benefit of overturn is clarity: "the strength of the law is a function, not only of the credibility of its creators, but also of its lucidity."[13] If the Supreme Court in evolving a particular doctrine (with respect to, for example, the commerce clause of article I, section 8), has made a premature statement about the meaning of a term, then lucidity calls for the present Supreme Court to overturn. If the law's character is evolutionary and "if the law has continuous, competing starting points for legal reasoning and they are equally authoritative, what is overruled in this process is the premature, the hasty generalization. . . . A premature formulation [an early precedent] on the part of a court is the beginning of this process."[14]

Clarity is consistent with judicial creativity and statesmanship. The Supreme Court's effort to rid the law of conflicting interpretations by cleansing the law through overturn has been a second justification for direct overturn by the highest court in America.

JUSTICE

Another justification for direct overturn of earlier precedent by the Supreme Court is the concept of justice. "In the last analysis, the decision whether to adhere to the policy of stare decisis or not is based on the effort to reconcile the need for certainty and uniformity with the requirement that justice be done."[15] Former Associate

Justice Arthur Goldberg's justification for overturn reflected this characteristic's importance.

Basic personal, civil, social, and political rights and liberties should expand to meet "new evils," Justice Goldberg argued. "Overruling is therefore permissible, or rather intrinsically necessary, to facilitate this beneficial expansion."[16] Stare decisis applies with an uneven force. When the Supreme Court attempts to overrule "in order to cut back the individual's fundamental constitutional protections against governmental interference, the commands of stare decisis are all but absolute"; yet when another Supreme Court majority "overrules to expand personal liberties" in order to achieve justice, stare decisis "interposes a markedly less restrictive caution."[17] For a number of justices on the Warren Court, the concept of justice and equity became a justification for overturning earlier precedents that denied Americans these fundamental rights.

THE POTENTIAL COSTS OF OVERTURN

Every political action—and judicial overturn of earlier Supreme Court decisions is a policy decision of a political actor—incurs costs. Judicial activism through direct overturn has the potential of eroding the credibility of the Court since public perceptions of the law "as man-made are sharpened when the law . . . appears to change so often."[18]

This potential dilemma is realized when new members of the Supreme Court view past judicial workmanship.

When a majority of a Court is suddenly reconstituted, there is likely to be a substantial unsettlement. There will be unsettlement until the new judges have taken their positions on constitutional doctrine. During that time, which may extend a decade or more, constitutional law may be in flux.[19]

When a newly constituted Court majority overturns an earlier Court's precedent, the majority of the Court doing the overturn has to create a judicial opinion that emphasizes sound reasoning. It must present good reasons to minimize potential political and professional criticisms.

A basic change in the law on a ground no firmer than a change in our membership invites the popular misconception that this institution is little different from the two political branches of the government. No misconception could do more lasting injury to this court and to the system of law which it is our abiding mission to serve.[20]

An opinion of the Supreme Court that poorly overturns an earlier judgment "botches the dispute-deciding function" and jeopardizes the status and legitimacy of the Supreme Court.[21]

The overturn opinion must be written so that major impersonal factors (rather than personal elements) dictate the necessity for the direct overturn. The Supreme Court justices can make dramatic reevaluations of the Constitution and construe the doctrine of stare decisis liberally if they join judicial creativity with judicial statesmanship. The benefits of overturn will outweigh the costs if the decision is based on reasons that are grounded in the fundamental principles of the American political and legal culture. As Archibald Cox put it: "The Court's power to give its decisions the force of legitimacy ultimately depends in large measure upon its professional artistry in weaving wise statecraft into the fabric of law."[22] In sum, an opinion that overturns an earlier precedent must be well written, thoroughly thought out, and based on an understanding of the fundamentals of the American legal system.

STANDARDS FOR OVERTURN

Some of the standards developed and elaborated upon by legal scholars with respect to the dilemmas of continuity and change in American law parallel the reasons offered by the judges for direct overturn of earlier opinions.

CHANGED CONDITIONS

New or changed social conditions or recent events that may have rendered an earlier precedent unfit is one justification suggested.[23] It is based on the premise that "law may grow to meet changing conditions and that the doctrine of stare decisis should not require a slavish adherence to authority where new conditions require new rules of conduct."[24] Reliance on this justification would permit an overrule opinion both "to reject a precedent and at the same time acknowledge its correctness when originally decided."[25]

EXAMINATION OF THE PRECEDENT

Some scholars suggest that the Court majority carefully examine the earlier opinion before overturning it.[26] Was it a divided decision, with a strong dissenting minority (such as *Hammer* v. *Dagenhart*)? Historically, has there been societal and legal support for the decision? Did later Court majorities use the earlier precedent consistently? Did it consistently provoke dissent? Was it distinguished (narrowed) by later Courts? These are some questions the Court majority should raise when discussing the possibility and necessity of overturning the earlier precedent.

PROCEDURAL CARE

Some suggest that a reasonable decision to overturn earlier precedent, all other justifications present, is one that devoted sufficient time for full argument and careful deliberation before deciding to overturn.[27] The Court should attempt to gauge the consequences if it overturns or fails to do so.

EXPERIENCE

This justification fits in well with the argument made by the justices themselves that overturn should take place when error is perceived. This argument goes directly to the theory of *democracy as fallibilism*.[28] It emphasizes the benefit of additional knowledge and practical experience in guiding the justices of the Supreme Court, fallible people, in the task of doing justice. The argument stresses that precedent must be rejected if the general principle has, in the words of Justice Brandeis, "failed to pass the test of experience, the trial and error process in the judicial function as well as in the physical sciences."[29]

Because of administrative difficulties with implementing an earlier opinion, lower court intransigence, or errors about facts or policy assumptions upon which the prior case, now precedent, was decided, that general principle has to be overturned.[30] "Years have brought about the doctrine that constitutional decisions must be tentative and subject to judicial cancellation if experience fails to verify them."[31]

INTENT OF THE FRAMERS

Before the Supreme Court overturns an earlier opinion, scholars advise it to examine the opinion carefully in light of the intent of the framers of the Constitution.[32] Is the prior decision consistent with the meaning intended by the language used in the Constitution? To answer this question accurately, the justices must have read the document in its entirety, must have understood the common meaning of the words in the Constitution, and understood the underlying circumstances surrounding the writing of those words in the document.[33] "Once the meaning of the clause has been ascertained, through an examination of the intent of the founders, the official oath taken by the judge precludes giving to any such provision a construction not warranted by the founders."[34]

REQUIREMENTS OF LATER PRECEDENT

Israel suggests that this is the justification the justices of the Supreme Court follow generally. The strategy is to indicate in the opinion that the general principle was being overturned "because of the 'error' of the earlier decision." Later decisions, also precedents, were inconsistent with the earlier ruling.[35]

The Court can use this strategy in two or three ways. Justices can acknowledge that the two sets of conflicting precedents could be reconciled but find it necessary to overturn "because the basis for the distinction between the cases was not justifiable in terms of the function of the legal principle involved."[36] Alternatively it can state that there was no way to reconcile the earlier opinion with the later judgments of the Court. The overruling decision, in this situation, is the "logical culmination of a gradual process of erosion."[37] The tide of later cases has forced the Court to overturn directly.

CONSISTENT WITH BASIC PRINCIPLES

The final argument that can be used to justify overturn opinions is that they are inconsistent with the basic principles of the ideal element, the Constitution.[38] These basic principles bind judges, litigants, and the legal profession; and if decisions are written so as to be in line with these enduring values, then the decision is not fiat but legitimate ruling by the court.

The faster pace of legal development would seem to create still greater need for striving to preserve, through the articulation of sound rationale, that sense of impartiality and continuity that gives legitimacy, and thus provides the sanction for the judgments of a court.[39]

OTHER JUSTIFICATIONS

Beyond these justifications, which scholars have classified as "necessary" overrulings,[40] there is another situation where an overturn by the Supreme Court is "justified": when a Supreme Court majority has a change of mind and the overturn is the reflection of this judicial change of mind "by the same judges of the Supreme Court."[41]

An unwarranted overturn by the Supreme Court, on the other hand, is a judgment of the court majority where: there has not been an adequate evaluation or due consideration of the reasoning in the earlier opinion, now overturned, nor has there been rigorous analysis of the consequences of the overturn opinion on the law; the Supreme Court has failed to give due weight to the values that are inherent in the consistency of the decision; and overruling results solely from changes in the Supreme Court makeup.[42]

There is extensive overlap between the justifications for overturn developed by the justices of the Supreme Court with those discussed by the legal scholars. Prior error is roughly analogous to the lessons of experience discussed by the scholars. Similarly clarity corresponds to changed conditions, history of the earlier decision, requirements of later precedent, and procedural care. Finally, the justice justification correlates with basic principles and the intent of the framers.

In sum, the standards for a reasonable overturn stress rightness, definiteness, and principle. Court judgments ought to be right rather than consistent or erroneous, definite rather than unclear and/or contradictory, and based on constitutional principles such as justice and equity. The legitimacy of the decision, however, depends on the manner in which it is written; it depends on the Court's professional artistry.

Direct overturning becomes art when the Court majority successfully justifies its action as based on impersonal factors and the reasons developed above rather than on sudden shifts of ideology and changes in makeup. The artistry consists of developing a line of judicial reasoning that borrows support from these reasons to explain the overturn. The important element is disguising the reality, uncertainty, with the fiction, stare decisis: overruling a decision "while purporting to follow the principles of stare decisis."[43]

Using these justifications carefully, the Court majority's overturn decision can blunt criticism of its action. A reasoned opinion of the Supreme Court is highly respected; a decree or fiat is condemned. To a certain extent, whether an opinion is reason or fiat is based on whose ox is gored. Beyond that reality, judicial opinions can be evaluated by examining the reasons for the Court's action.

JUDICIAL STATESMANSHIP IN DIRECT OVERTURN OPINIONS

Because of the reality of the law's uncertainty, judicial decision making involves judicial discretion. To a certain extent, given the wide room for movement, "judicial predispositions largely determine the direction of decision."[44] Three factors guide, influence and motivate the actions of judges in their professional behavior: social attitudes, social institutions, and their understanding of the legal norms. The interaction of these forces creates the objective reality for the judge.[45]

Each judge will react differently to precedents and the precedential value of past decisions of the Supreme Court. The decision to overturn or not, to follow precedent or not, is, finally, a matter of each justice's drawing upon a "complex of habits, experiences, and skills" that come from his understanding of the taught traditions of the law, the place of the Supreme Court in American society, and life itself.[46]

One assumption about overturning of earlier precedent has been that appointees to the Supreme Court who have had prior judicial experience would be less prone to overturning opinions. Their prior experience, the argument goes, "generates self-restraint and recognition of the need for stability in decision making."[47] Such a notion, according to a political scientist who examined the background of all the Supreme Court justices who participated in direct overturns, going back to the very first overturn (*Hudson* v. *Guestier*, 1810, overturning *Rose* v. *Himely*, 1808), "that such experience predisposes one to adhere to stare decisis is clearly without foundation."[48] On the contrary, argues Schmidhauser, prior judicial experience "provides a degree of psychic security to justices who were thoroughly integrated into the American common-law judicial tradition."[49] Taking into consideration earlier judicial experiences, emphasizing result orientedness and discretion, "86% of the 29 Justices of the Court with such prior experience showed a strong propensity to abandon stare decisis than did the Justices lacking such experience (69% of 42 jurists)."[50]

Typically prior judicial experience is inversely related to strict adherence of former decisions of the Supreme Court: "Justices lacking this background may tend to overcompensate by more rigid adherence to stare decisis."[51] Furthermore the typical dissenter, according to Schmidhauser, is a "tenacious advocate of traditional legal doctrines which were being abandoned during his tenure. He adhered to precedent with a far greater regularity than his non dissenting colleagues."[52]

Most Supreme Court justices, therefore, will express different attitudes toward the value of stare decisis and the necessity of overturning precedent. Depending on his experiences he will vary from the neo-result-oriented jurist (such as Justice William O. Douglas) to the self-admitted principle-oriented jurist (such as Justice Felix Frankfurter or Justice John M. Harlan II). Douglas believed there was very little room in constitutional adjudication for stare decisis; for him, all constitutional questions remained open. Frankfurter's view was that the Constitution was the ultimate touchstone of constitutionality and that reversals of earlier constitutional cases could occur "by the orderly process of law and should not derive from mere private judgment."[53]

The essence of Frankfurter's position, which differed from the Douglas extreme and the philosophy of Hugo Black (which stressed literalism in constitutional adjudication),[54] was if overturns by judges and courts are to be effective and respected, they must "draw their sanction from a continuing community of principle."[55]

Essentially this perception forms the basis of the statesmanlike overturn. For an overturn decision of the Supreme Court to be reasonable and principled, rather than fiat and decree, certain elements of judicial craftsmanship must be present. First, a reasoned overturn opinion adapts the Constitution to changing social and economic conditions that earlier judicial decisions could not have foreseen. This is the element referred to earlier as *clarity, error,* and *fallibilism.*

A second element is respect for the fixed political and constitutional principles such as liberty, due process, equality under law, and, the central value, justice. A good overturn does not "abandon the vision of the founding fathers."[56] I have referred to this as *justice, intent of the framers,* and *basic principles.*

Finally, while the statesmanlike opinion of the Court overturns earlier decisions in the light of *changing conditions* in the society, it seeks to inform the litigants, and the society as a whole, of the principled reasons for that overturn.

The Supreme Court justices in this manner serve as a continuous constitutional convention. Optimally they will function in a reasoned, principled manner when they overturn in order to adapt the constitutional principles to new ages and new problems. This task "requires the political sensitivity of the statesman as well as the doctrinal skills of the lawyer."[57]

THREE CASE STUDIES

In the attempt to observe whether standards inherent in reasonable, principled overturn decisions by the Supreme Court discussed above have been employed by the justices when they actually overturned, three situations will be examined carefully.

The first overturn to be examined (in chapter 3) will be the 1941 decision of a New Deal, liberal Supreme Court: *United States* v.

Darby Lumber Company, 312 U.S. 100, overturning *Hammer* v. *Dagenhart*, 247 U.S. 251 (1918). The second overturn to be examined (chapter 4) will be *West Virginia Board of Education* v. *Barnette*, 319 U.S. 624 (1943), overturning *Minersville School District* v. *Gobitis*, 310 U.S. 586 (1940). The final overturn (chapter 5) decision that will be examined is *Hudgens* v. *National Labor Relations Board*, 96 S.C. Reporter 1029 (1976), overturning *Amalgamated Food Employees Union Local 590* v. *Logan Valley Plaza*, 391 U.S. 308 (1968).

In the first case, an allegedly liberal court majority overturned an opinion of what is considered to be a conservative majority. In the third overturn a conservative court majority, the so-called Nixon Court, overturned an opinion written during the Warren Court era, the "first liberal activist Court in our history."[58] The second overturn presents the unusual situation of a Supreme Court majority's changing its mind and overturning its own earlier opinion.

SUMMARY

The law in America is not uniform, certain, and stable. Conflicting standards of law and uncertainty presented to courts in litigation in the form of conflicting facts, conflicting law, and conflicting principles are factors that judges confront all the time. Judges live with this uncertainty and, balancing demands, determine the direction of the law. Yet there is a persistent demand for stability and continuity in law. Thus judicial changes in the law must be craftsmanlike, statesmanlike actions because of this need to maintain continuity in the legal system. The statesmanlike overturn must balance continuity and change.

Critical justifications for direct overturn include error, fallibilism, clarity, and justice: rightness, definiteness, and principle. If overturn incurs costs because of its visibility, these costs will be minimal if the Court artistically weaves into its decision legitimate reasons for its dramatic action.

Although Supreme Court justices bring with them to the Court various life experiences that they draw on for guidance in the decision-making function, the assumption that undergirds the reasonable overturn decision is that judgments will transcend the personal dimension. "Constitutional doctrines necessarily change and precedents are necessarily overruled, yet this must be accomplished with due regard for the necessary demands of continuity and with constant attention to the political and social consequences of each decision."[59]

NOTES

1. J. Braxton Craven, "Paean to Pragmatism," *North Carolina Law Review* 50 (1971): 978.

2. William Blackstone, "Justice and Legal Reasoning," *William and Mary Law Review* 18 (Winter 1976): 334. "To overrule an important precedent is serious business. It calls for sober appraisal of the disadvantages of the innovation as well as those of the questioned case, a weighing of practical effects of one against the other." Robert H. Jackson, "Decisional Law and Stare Decisis," *American Bar Association Journal* 30 (March 1944): 334.

3. John R. Schmidhauser, "Stare Decisis, Dissent, and the Background of the Justices of the Supreme Court of the United States," *University of Toronto Law Journal* 14 (September 1962): 196.

4. Gerold Israel, "Gideon v. Wainright: The 'Art' of Overruling," in P. Kurland, ed., *The Supreme Court Review, 1963* (Chicago: University of Chicago Press, 1963), pp. 217-18.

5. Albert Blaustein and Andrew Field, " 'Overruling' Opinions in the Supreme Court," *Michigan Law Review* 57 (December 1958): 166.

6. *Norvell* v. *Illinois,* 366 U.S. 211 (1961).

7. *Boys Market* v. *Retail Clerks Union,* 398 U.S. 235 (1970).

8. Leon Sachs, "Stare Decisis and the Legal Tender Cases," *Virginia Law Review* 20 (1934): 856-857; Stanley Reed, "Stare Decisis and Constitutional Law," *Pennsylvania Bar Association Quarterly* 33 (October 1937): 138; Charlotte Bernhardt, "Supreme Court Reversals on Constitutional Issues," *Cornell Law Quarterly* 34 (1948): 67; E. M. Wise, "The Doctrine of Stare Decisis," *Wayne Law Review* 21 (July 1975): 1058.

9. Wendell Brown, "Construing the Constitution: A Trial Lawyer's Plea for Stare Decisis," *American Bar Association Journal* 44 (August 1958): 743.

10. *Burnet* v. *Corondao Oil and Gas Co.,* 285 U.S. 393 (1932).

11. *Mitchell* v. *W. T. Grant Co.,* 40 L. Ed. 2d 406 (1974).

12. Blaustein and Field, op. cit., p. 183.

13. "Lower Court Disavowal of Supreme Court Precedent," *Virginia Law Review* 60 (1974): 514.

14. Roscoe Pound, Symposium, "The Status of the Rule of Judicial

Precedent," *University of Cincinnati Law Review* 14 (March 1940): 330-331.

15. Bernhardt, op. cit., p. 68.

16. Arthur J. Goldberg, *Equal Justice: The Warren Court Era of the Supreme Court* (New York: Farrar, Straus, and Giroux, 1971), p. 85.

17. Ibid., p. 74.

18. *Virginia Law Review*, "Lower Court Disavowal," p. 513.

19. William O. Douglas, "Stare Decisis," *Columbia Law Review* 49 (June 1949): 402-403.

20. *Mitchell* v. *W. T. Grant*, 406.

21. Leflar, op. cit., p. 336.

22. Wise, op. cit., p. 1059.

23. Israel, "The Art of Overruling," p. 217.

24. Justice Owen Roberts, in *Mahnich* v. *Southern Steamship Co.*, 321 U.S. 96 (1944): 113.

25. Israel, op. cit., p. 220.

26. See Noland, op. cit., and Jackson, op. cit.

27. Ibid.

28. See, generally, Thomas Thorson, *The Logic of Democracy* (New York: Norton and Company, 1961).

29. *Burnet* v. *Corondado Oil Company*, 285 U.S. 393 (1932).

30. See "Lower Court Disavowals," 499-500.

31. "The Task of Maintaining Our Liberties," *American Bar Association Journal* (1953): 961, 962.

32. Brown, op. cit., p. 745; Gary Jacobsohn, "Constitutional Adjudication and Judicial Statesmanship," *Emory Law Journal* 23 (Winter 1974): 142.

33. Jacobsohn, op. cit.

34. Ibid., p. 141.

35. Israel, op. cit., p. 223. See Howard Ball, *The Vision and the Dream of Justice Hugo Black* (University: University of Alabama Press, 1975), for an examination of Justice Black's judicial views on this subject.

36. Ibid., p. 224.

37. Ibid., p. 225.

38. Blackstone, op. cit., p. 345; Wise, op. cit., p. 1058.

39. Wise, op. cit., p. 1057.

40. Blaustein and Field, op. cit., p. 168.

41. Ibid., p. 174.

42. Ibid., p. 176.

43. "Statesmanship is where an enduring principle is affirmed in the opinion even if the decision might suggest that it has been violated." Jacobsohn,

op. cit., p. 148. Israel, op. cit., p. 226.

44. Lionel Frankel, "Humanist Law: The Need for Change in Legal Education—or—If Judges Do Not Find the Law, but Make It, What Do They Make It from?" *Utah Law Review*, no. 1 (1976): 41

45. David Dittfurth, "Judicial Reasoning and Social Change," *Indiana Law Journal* 50 (Winter 1975): 261.

46. Wise, op. cit., p. 1052.

47. Schmidhauser, op. cit., p. 194.

48. Ibid., p. 209.

49. Ibid., p. 202.

50. Ibid.

51. Ibid., p. 210.

52. Ibid., p. 211.

53. Noland, op. cit., p. 112.

54. See Ball, *Vision and the Dream*.

55. Wise, op. cit., p. 1058.

56. Jacobsohn, op. cit., p. 149.

57. Jan G. Deutsch, "Neutrality, Legitimacy, and the Supreme Court: Some Intersections between Law and Political Science," *Stanford Law Review* 20 (1968): 240.

58. Leonard Levy, *The Supreme Court under Earl Warren* (New York: Quadrangle Books, 1972), p. 16.

59. Noland, op. cit., p. 126.

3 The Child Labor Case and Overturn

"Congress shall have power to regulate commerce with foreign nations, and among the several states." The commerce clause of the Constitution (article 1, section 8), is one of the general grants of power whose definition is not found in the logic or the language of the Constitution. Judges had to decide the direction of its meaning from an understanding of the essential character of that legislative power. In a case or controversy before the Supreme Court dealing with the meaning of the clause, the solution regarding whether a congressional prohibition in law is a regulation of interstate commerce "depends upon a legal judgement as to what is best, as does the decision of most constitutional questions."[1]

In this process of determining the meaning of constitutional clauses, craftsmanship and judicial statesmanship require careful examination of the basic principles behind the clauses in the Constitution and an updating of earlier Court judgments in light of changing conditions in the society. This chapter focuses on the actions of the Supreme Court with respect to actions of Congress based on a legislative reading of the commerce clause. In order to place the child labor case, *Hammer* v. *Dagenhart* (1918), and the overturn decision, *United States* v. *Darby Lumber Company* (1941), in perspective, the first section of the chapter will provide historical background.

THE POWER OF CONGRESS TO REGULATE COMMERCE TO *HAMMER*, 1918

During the period immediately following the Revolutionary war, the Articles of Confederation period (1781-1789), the thirteen states dealt with each other economically in a manner that necessitated demands for a national power over commercial activities. States taxed each other's imports just as they taxed goods coming from abroad. Certain "fundamental changes were needed," and commercial interests called for amending the Articles so that a central government would be given power to promote industry and commerce at home. This change meant the takeover from the sovereign states of the regulation of interstate commerce in order to break down and prohibit commercial barriers among the states.² "The primary purpose in granting to the Congress (in the 1787 Constitution) the power to regulate commerce among the states was the desire to avoid the burdensome restrictions which rapidly developed in the period immediately following the revolution."³

At the 1787 Philadelphia convention, the delegates accepted the following view without much adverse criticism on at least three separate occasions in May and August:

The national congress shall be permitted to legislate in all cases for the general interests of the nation, and also in those to which the states are separately incompetent, or in which the harmony of the United States may be interrupted by the exercise of individual legislation.⁴

This attitude of the convention delegates became the essence of the Constitution's commerce clause. Commerce was the only one of the enumerated powers in which the Congress was given a broad power to regulate trade and business. One scholar wrote that

the convention must have understood that in that clause it was granting to Congress all the power over trade or business which the national government would need to possess to provide for situations which the states separately would be unable to meet. In view of the fact that centralized commercial regulation was universally recognized as the primary reason for preparing a new Constitution, the convention would not have been likely to have meant the commerce clause to have a narrow or restrictive meaning.⁵

The first Supreme Court pronouncement on the meaning of the commerce clause in the 1824 case *Gibbons* v. *Ogden* reflected this expansive view of the power to regulate commerce. Chief Justice John Marshall, in one of his most important decisions, said that the commerce power is a plenary power of the national government; that it is the power to prescribe the rule by which commerce is to be governed; that there are no limits, other than those in the Constitution itself, to the power of the national government to regulate commerce. Commerce, he wrote, is "intercourse—commercial intercourse," and that term encompasses trade, traffic, navigation, and "every species of commercial intercourse" comprehended. It is the congressional power to regulate, to make rules to govern this commercial intercourse. It is, he wrote, "a power complete in itself."[6] In sum, his view was that the commerce power reached all commercial matters affecting the states generally: the congressional power over commerce, foreign or domestic, was that of only the centralized government.[7]

Until the passage of the Interstate Commerce Act in 1887 and the Sherman Anti-Trust Act in 1890, there was no substantial use of the power of the national government inherent in the commerce clause according to John Marshall. With the rapid and haphazard growth of the economy in the period of rapid industrialization after the Civil War, which the states did little to control, some Americans demanded national control of such unregulated economic expansionism. Workers demanded help from a growing integrated, nationwide economy that was not affected by state actions.

These calls for national regulation to limit and regulate economic activity must be seen in light of the other tendency that grew up next to the Marshall perspective on national power: the Madisonian notion of dual federalism.[8] This countervailing attitude expressed a fear of an unlimited extension of national power and supremacy that would turn state governments into meaningless appendages of the central government. Madison's view of the issue, expressed in 1819, was that the coexistence of the states with their powers inherent in the Tenth Amendment, the reserved or police powers of the state, was itself a basic limit on the powers of the national government.[9]

To the dual federalists, the Constitution developed a governmental system that had two locuses of power and two spheres of governmental activity: national activity limited to the enumerated powers of the Constitution and state activity based on the inherent police powers that all sovereign entities had as a consequence of their sovereignty: "Collision is not contemplated as a rule of life of the system, but the contrary."[10] On the power to regulate commerce, dual federalists believed that the power of the national government was not plenary and that it was confronted by the police powers of the state at every turn. "The commerce power was for the promotion and advancement of commerce; it was not a power to strike commerce down for the advancement of other purposes."[11]

These tendencies first collided in 1903 in the important case of *Champion* v. *Ames.*[12] The Congress had used the commerce power to prohibit from interstate commerce the importation, mailing, or interstate carriage of lottery tickets. The Federal Lottery Act was challenged on the grounds that this type of prohibition was reserved to the states under the Tenth Amendment and that the commerce clause did not contemplate national prohibition of goods from interstate traffic. In a closely divided five-to-four opinion, the Supreme Court reasoned that the congressional power to regulate interstate commerce included the power to prohibit commerce. Quoting John Marshall, the majority reaffirmed the view that the power of Congress to regulate is plenary and is subject to no limitation except such as may be found in the Constitution itself. "Congress has . . . only legislated in respect of a matter which concerns the people of the United States." Congress alone, the opinion concluded, "has the power to occupy, by legislation, the whole field of interstate commerce."[13]

The dissenters, led by Chief Justice Melville Fuller, argued that the Tenth Amendment prohibited the Congress from legislating in this area: "The power to suppress lotteries belongs to the states and not to the Congress." The argument was based on dual federalism. Until 1918 (in *Hammer*), it remained a minority view with respect to the use of the commerce power, with the exception of *E. C. Knight* (1895) and others like it that raised the question of whether manufacturing was commerce and thus subject to regulation by the Congress.[14]

From the *Champion* case to *Hammer*, (1903-1918), the Supreme

Court majority consistently validated numerous legislative enactments of the Congress that employed the commerce clause to prohibit certain items of commerce to move in interstate commerce. The lottery ticket case set the pattern for the Court: in determining whether the legislation constitutes a regulation of commerce, its character was determined by looking to the field of operation, not to the purpose or motive of its enactment.[15]

Until *Hammer*, exclusions from interstate commerce included: lottery tickets, obscene material,[16] white slave traffic,[17] impure, unwholesome, adulterated food or drugs,[18] misbranded products,[19] diseased plants and animals,[20] and intoxicating liquors.[21] During this time a "national police power [developed] under the Commerce Clause . . . by which the channels of interstate commerce have been closed to commodities which are injurious, not to that commerce or to any of the agencies or facilities thereof, but to the health, safety, morals, and general welfare of the nation."[22]

Until 1918, the Court had held to the Marshall view of commerce: that the congressional power to regulate commerce was plenary and preempted the field and could be used to restrict items from the free flow of interstate commerce. Thus next to the state police power grew a national police power; the Supreme Court dissenters, aware of the Madisonian concern about centralized power-trammeling state powers, continued to argue that such legislation violated the Constitution. In the child labor case, their fears became the law.

THE CHILD LABOR CASE, *HAMMER* v. *DAGENHART* (1918)

FACTS AND CONSTITUTIONAL ISSUES

In 1916 the Congress passed the Child Labor Act in an attempt to deal with the "socially unwise and morally repugnant issue"[23] of young children who worked fifty to sixty hours a week in mines, factories, and mills. The act prohibited the transportation in interstate commerce of goods made at a factory in which, within thirty days prior to their removal from work, children under fourteen had been employed or children between fourteen and sixteen had worked more than eight hours in a day, more than six days a week, or after 7 P.M. and before 6 A.M. A manufacturer who so employed such children was prohibited from shipping goods to other states. After abiding by the requirements of the act for thirty days, the owner could then ship merchandise in interstate commerce and could again use the channels of interstate commerce so long as he continued to adhere to the standards of employment outlined in the Child Labor Act.

Homer Dagenhart, the father of two sons employed in a cotton mill, one younger than fourteen and the other between fourteen and sixteen, filed suit in the U.S. District Court in North Carolina asking the court to enjoin enforcement of the act. The district court held the act unconstitutional and entered a decree enjoining its enforcement. The government appealed the judgment to the Supreme Court.

In defense of the act of Congress, the Justice Department's arguments before the Supreme Court emphasized four basic points:

1) Congress can control transportation and the Act distinguishes between manufacturing and interstate movement. The manufacturer can continue to employ children, but cannot move his goods in interstate commerce; the 10th Amendment reserve powers of a state do not begin until the power of Congress leaves off—there is no encroachment of the state's police powers.

2) Labor per se is not inherently bad; the evil effects of child labor, with growth of industrial activity become manifest. Physical well being suffers; physical growth stunted by night work and excessive hours; child becomes dwarfed in mind and body. The goodness or badness of the product of child labor was irrelevant; we judge goodness and badness by their effect.

3) Interstate commerce conception is a practical one, drawn from the course of business. Differences in states' laws, even slight, alter the development of an industry. No state can use the channels of interstate commerce for unfair competition. States cannot handle this dilemma, only the congress can.

4) The Act is legitimate because it was passed for the public health a) in states competing with the point of origin state and b) in the producing state itself. Congress can legitimately legislate to prevent the evils resulting from the interstate transportation of child made goods.[24]

The arguments of the solicitor general reflected the Marshall view of the commerce power: plenary and without limits except for those in the Constitution. The fact that interstate commerce, a power of the Congress, was in question meant that the Tenth Amendment argument was irrelevant, for the states have no coextensive power or sovereignty with respect to interstate transportation.

Counsel for Dagenhart held that the act was unconstitutional. Their argument before the Supreme Court, reflecting the Madisonian fear of a strong central government, had four essential themes:

1) The purpose of the Act was to prevent the employment of children and not to promote commerce or the interests of the states into which the child made goods were sent. Congress may prevent the facility of interstate commerce from being made an instrument of evil but the subject regulated must be related to interstate commerce. In this Act, there is no relationship between the thing regulated (innocent harmless products) and the object to be attained (child labor protections in all states).

2) The congressional power to regulate interstate commerce does not reach back to prohibit harmless, useful goods because of the pre-commerce condition of labor. Before or after transit, the things moved are beyond the legitimate control of congress.

3) Child labor was subject only to the police powers of the state through employment of 10th Amendment powers. Congress has no general police power. If it absorbs the police powers of the state, what is left to the states?

4) Congress cannot regulate commerce for the promotion of what is deemed by a transient majority to be the welfare of the people. The right to create, work, and transport is essential to the citizen and the welfare of the country. It has a fundamental protection that congress cannot abridge.[25]

The argument emphasized that the congressional power to regulate interstate commerce, unlike the regulation of foreign commerce, was limited because of the sovereignty of the states. The federal system prevented Congress from using the commerce power to regulate an activity that fell within the province of the states. The view was narrow; the federalism it espoused was a dual federalism where the Congress and the states operated in separate spheres of activity. In this case, Congress contravened the reserved powers of the state by regulating an area, child labor, that all states had dealt with prior to 1916.

THE OPINIONS

The Majority Opinion: Mr. Justice Day

The Court majority of five justices (four dissented) broke with the past judgments of the Supreme Court by distinguishing *Hammer* from the earlier acts of Congress validated by the Court. The controlling question for the Court in *Hammer* was whether the act was within the authority of Congress under the commerce clause. "The power," wrote Day, "is one to control the means by which commerce is carried on, which is directly the contrary of the assumed right to forbid commerce from moving and thus destroy it as to particular commodities." (A basic question must be raised here: if Congress is given the power to control, why is forbidding commerce "directly contrary"?) The Court majority stated that Congress cannot forbid movement of "ordinary commodities" in interstate commerce.

Prior cases had dealt with goods that were evil; the character of the particular subjects was the basis of earlier Supreme Court rulings that had validated these acts. In all these cases, involving lottery tickets, white slave trade, impure foods and drugs, and so forth, "the use of interstate commerce was necessary to the accomplishment of harmful results. . . . This element is wanting in the present case."

Looking into the purpose and motives of the Congress, the Supreme Court stated that "the thing intended to be accomplished by this Act is the denial of the facilities of interstate commerce to those manufacturers in the states who employ children within the prohibited ages. The Act . . . aims to standardize the ages at which children may be employed in mining and manufacturing within the states."

Day then accepted the argument of Dagenhart's counsel and concluded that making goods and mining coal are not commerce, "nor does the fact that these things are to be afterwards shipped or used in interstate commerce, make their production a part thereof." The production of articles intended for interstate commerce is a matter of local regulation, the Court majority reasoned. Commerce begins only when the product is actually delivered to a common carrier for transportation, not before.

Separating production from commerce was necessary for the Court majority because of their fears, analogous to the Madisonian fear, of the consequences.

If it were otherwise, all manufacture intended for interstate commerce shipment would be brought under federal control to the practical exclusion of the authority of the states, a result certainly not contemplated by the framers of the Constitution when they vested in Congress the authority to regulate commerce among the states.

Congress cannot use the commerce clause to equalize working conditions; this is a power the states have, if they wish to use it. Congress can only regulate commerce; it does not have authority to control the states in their exercise of the police power over local trade and manufacture.

The Court majority concluded its opinion by discussing the police powers of the states under the Tenth Amendment. Congress can regulate only a "purely federal matter"; it was not given the power to destroy local powers carefully reserved to the states by the Tenth Amendment. The Court essentially propounded a dual federalistic stance: "In interpreting the Constitution it must never be forgotten that the nation is made up of states to which are entrusted the powers of local government. And to them and to the people the powers not expressly delegated to the national government are reserved." In its eagerness to make the case for dual federalism, the majority added *expressly* to the Tenth Amendment, a word that had been discussed when the Amendments were discussed in Congress but had been left out by the framers of the Bill of Rights. In artificially separating local from national powers and controls, the majority reached the conclusion that the act was an unconstitutional infringement of state powers by the national government: "This Court has no more important function that that which devolves upon it the obligation to preserve inviolate the constitutional limitations upon the exercise of authority, federal and state, to the end that each may continue to discharge, harmoniously with the other, the duties entrusted to it by the Constitution."

Thus the Child Labor Act was held unconstitutional for two reasons: "it transcends the authority delgated to Congress over commerce but also exerts a power as to a purely local matter to which the federal authority does not extend." The Court thereupon affirmed the decree of the U.S. District Court enjoining the enforcement of the Child Labor Act of 1916.

The Dissenting Opinion: Mr. Justice Holmes

For the four dissenters the basic question was whether the Constitution gave the Congress the power to prohibit shipment in interstate commerce of any product of a cotton mill situated in the United States. The Child Labor Act confined itself to prohibiting the carriage of certain goods in interstate commerce; the power to regulate includes the power to prohibit—and Congress has the power to regulate (prohibit) commerce "in unqualified terms." The statute, then, was "clearly within the Congress's constitutional power."

The question is then narrowed to whether, in its exercise of an otherwise constitutional power, the act should be declared unconstitutional because of its impact on the conduct of states. The answer was readily apparent:

I should have thought that the most conspicuous decisions of this court had made it clear that the power to regulate commerce and other constitutional powers could not be cut down or qualified by the fact that it might interfere with the carrying out of the domestic policy of any state.

Reminiscent of the great Marshall opinions expanding the powers of the national government, the dissenting opinion of Justice Holmes emphasized the supremacy of the national government when it conflicted with state governments in the area of commerce. To separate production from transportation is a matter of semantics, argued the dissenters: "It does not matter whether the supposed evil precedes or follows the transportation, It is enough that in the opinion of Congress the transportation encourages the evil."

The Holmes dissent was critical of the majority's examination of Congress's motive in the Child Labor Act: "I had thought that the propriety of the exercise of a power admitted to exist in some cases was for consideration of Congress alone and that this Court always had disavowed the right to intrude its judgment upon questions of policies or morals." The dissent concluded by stating the obvious: when a state seeks to send its products across the state line, these products become interstate commerce. Under the Constitution such commerce belongs not to the states but to the Congress alone to regulate."

Holmes's conclusion focused on the fact that the Congress was responsible for legislating on behalf of the entire nation, and the perspective in the national legislature might very well be different from that of North Carolina (or any other state): "The national welfare as understood by Congress may require a different attitude within its sphere from that of some self-seeking state. It seems to me entirely constitutional for Congress to enforce its understanding by all means possible."

In sum, the dissenters held that what was being regulated was material that moved in commerce, interstate commerce. The national Congress has the plenary power, not shared by the states, to regulate—prohibit if necessary—interstate commerce. There was no discrimination for all goods of the same class; those manufactured by children in violation of the Child Labor Act were alike prohibited. Judges must not interject their fears and their prejudices into the act of constitutional adjudication, stated the dissenters—pointing to the fact that that was exactly what the five-man majority had done in *Hammer* v. *Dagenhart.*

EVALUATION AND IMPACT OF *HAMMER* v. *DAGENHART*

Evaluation

Although some supported the Court decision especially that portion of the business community that employed children extensively, most of the press were highly critical of the Day judgment.[26] The majority opinion's three propositions were soundly condemned by educators, legal scholars, and others on grounds of ignorance of economic realities, judicial fiat, and illogical reasoning. The basic tenets of the opinion were:

1. The act was not a regulation of commerce among the states because the items prohibited were not evil or would not lead to evil ends.

2. The act was an invasion of the reserved powers of the states.

3. The act was inimical to the federal system that the Constitution established and maintains.

A defender of the majority opinion, Andrew Bruce, underlined the Court's fear of unrestrained national power that had led to the issuance of judicial fiat in the decision. He criticized Justice Holmes's dissent, arguing that if it had been the majority opinion, it would have allowed the development of a national dictatorship of economic and social policies, all without judicial review of such national action.

A temporary political majority, gathered in Washington, D.C., utterly ignorant of local and economic conditions of the states, would superimpose its conception of public policy upon all of the states, destroying their industry, control social policy, and over the exercise of these powers there would be no judicial control.[27]

This attitude—fear of majoritarianian democracy in the Congress and the impact of such legislative energies upon the states—was the basis for the majority judgment.

"Laissez-fairism and the desire to preserve state's rights led to the holding."[28] This fear, accompanied by the parallel one that the states would lose all their powers to the federal government, led the five-man majority to rule the act invalid.[29] For some legal commentators, this was simply judicial fiat on behalf of dual federalism. Influenced by their personal predilections on a question of policy, the five judges invalidated it. The five looked into the intentions and aims of the Congress rather than at whether the Constitution gave the national legislature the power to regulate commerce in that fashion.[30] In the attempt to avoid such national initiatives, the majority distinguished between production and transportation in order to invalidate the Child Labor Act.

A second criticism of the majority opinion is that production and transportation to markets "are so joined together by economic nexus that no man, court, or legislature can put them asunder."[31] The opportunity to market and have markets available is a necessary condition of production. The Court majority, artificially separating the two, created a judicial decision whose vital defect was its "sheer anachronism."[32]

The Court majority did not comprehend the changing conditions of commerce in America in the industrialized twentieth century. Production, wrote one critic of the opinion, had become tied to an interstate market, a market whose characteristics and activities ignored the existence of state lines. "Commerce is not transportation from one state to another—it is traffic, an onward coursing stream of business which knows no state lines."[33] The majority's distinction between activities that precede and those that follow transportation is "a pure invention of the judicial mind."[34] The reality of commerce and transportation and business activities in the twentieth century suggests that states cannot cope with many business activities that formerly were manageable. In judging that commerce began when the carrier assumed control of the product, the majority on the Court were drawing upon a fictitious view of business activity.

A much more obvious error was that the majority ignored the fact that once a product is sent across the state line, it is an object in interstate commerce and subject to congressional regulation. No matter how much the Day opinion stressed the difference between production and transportation, the fact was that Congress was regulating goods in interstate commerce. The Constitution, in its generality, did not furnish a description of the kinds of commerce that Congress could regulate. But no one can doubt that the act prohibited commercial movement of a class of products. Such a regulation of commerce cannot be, logically, an exercise of a power reserved to the states by virtue of the Tenth Amendment.

Still other criticisms of the Day opinion were that it was "superfluous,"[35] "logically indefensible,"[36] and contained "palpable blunders, fallacious reasoning, and unreasoned assertions."[37] The conclusion that the act violated the Tenth Amendment, to another writer, "neglects history, logic, and judicial precedents."[38] For example, the distinction between illicit and licit goods drawn by Justice Day, is indefensible. As the solicitor general argued before the Court, the goodness or badness of an item is determined by how society views the item and its effects on people in society. For example, someone determined that liquor is morally reprehensible; and the Webb-Kenyon Act, passed by Congress and validated by the Supreme Court, made liquor an evil. In sum, the "illicitness of goods depends entirely on the mores of society as defined by the Congress."[39] The logic of *Hammer*, according to another critic of the majority decision, is that a state can insist that the channels of interstate commerce can and must remain open for the carriage of its products—and the state can resist other states and the restraints of the national Congress in its efforts to use the channels of commerce.[41] In this reasoning the power of Congress to regulate commerce "among the states" is entirely forgotten.

In short, the majority, evidently in the name of dual federalism, prohibited Congress from regulating commerce. It interposed its views for those of the national legislature. To protect the domestic policy of the state of North Carolina the constitutional power to regulate commerce was, in the words of Justice Holmes, "cut down and qualified." The Supreme Court annulled an act of Congress because five judges thought the Congress had gone too far.

THE IMPACT

Hammer had tremendous impact in the policy area it negated: child labor laws. Edward Corwin, a noted constitutional scholar, and others have maintained that *Hammer* changed dual federalism to triple federalism with respect to the problem of child labor: national government, state government, and "no government." *Hammer* created a governmental vacuum: Congress could not deal with child labor; states could not prohibit products manufactured by child labor from entering their states if the product was harmless and innocent.[41] The result was an effective shackling of the states and the national government in an effort to prevent unfair competition in the labor market.

Other commentators argued that outside of the issue policy concern of child labor, the *Hammer* opinion, from the day it was written, was a "misfit."[42] Because of the powerful dissent of Justice Holmes and the overwhelming amount of criticism from the legal journals, as well as the poor features of the opinion itself, *Hammer* as precedent was ineffective and was limited to its own facts by subsequent cases. Not only did it break with past precedent; it was not well received and was immediately distinguished by the Supreme Court after it was announced.[43] After it was written, Congress successfully prohibited from interstate commerce articles not evil in themselves such as stolen automobiles, unregistered investment securities, and tobacco in excess of quotas established by the Congress for farmers within individual states.[44]

Some even maintain that the 1937 Supreme Court decision in *Kentucky Whip and Collar Company* v. *Illinois Central Railroad Company*[45] dramatically narrowed the scope of *Hammer*, if not silently overturning the child labor case.[46] The opinion sustained a federal law that forbade the shipment of convict-made goods into a state forbidding their sale. *Hammer* was distinguished because, the Court reasoned in 1937, it attempted to regulate labor at the local production level, whereas in *Kentucky Whip and Collar* the legislation was designed to prevent the use of interstate commerce channels to cause "harmful results" and "effect the evil intended."[47] It was a crude distinction at best, but the Court in 1937 was undergoing great stress and possibly was not yet ready to overturn *Hammer*. In 1938, however, the Congress presented the Supreme Court with an opportunity to reconsider the viability of *Hammer* when it passed—and the president signed—the Fair Labor Standards Act.

THE OVERTURN OF HAMMER: *UNITED STATES* v. *DARBY* (1941)

FACTS AND CONSTITUTIONAL ISSUES

The Roosevelt administration between 1933 and 1938 introduced over a dozen major pieces of legislation in the attempt to ameliorate the problems created by the depression: bank and business failures, severe unemployment, production cutbacks, dramatic declines in farm and labor income, farm and home mortgage foreclosures. The Roosevelt New Deal strategy was to use the powers of the national government forcefully to gain the recovery Americans desperately needed. Measures such as the Agricultural Adjustment Acts, the National Industrial Recovery Act, the Bituminous Coal Conservation Act, the Social Security Act, the Farm Mortgage Act, the Municipal Bankruptcy Act, the Railway Pension Act, and the Fair Labor Standards Act were introduced during this period to deal with the economic problems.

In this national attack on the economic crisis, the Roosevelt administration saw in the commerce clause the legitimation of its actions, for that enumerated power was "most directly concerned with business and economic, or commercial matter."[48] The question uppermost on the minds of the lawyers in the New Deal administration was whether the commerce clause "could bear the load" given the existence of a Supreme Court majority that still adhered to a formal distinction between production and manufacturing and transportation in interstate commerce.[49]

The Congress passed the various pieces of legislation based on reality of a nationwide market and possessing the Marshall view of the power of interstate commerce in the hands of Congress. The Supreme Court, however, in a series of momentous five-to-four decisions, invalidated most of the legislation.[50]

After his reelection in 1936 and after his programs had been invalidated by the Supreme Court, President Roosevelt introduced his Court-packing plan to the nation in 1937. It was an ingenious attempt to add six more justices to the Supreme Court, all appointed by President Roosevelt who, after five years as president, had appointed none. After great publicity and fanfare, the plan failed to clear the Senate. It did, however, make an impact on the justices themselves; shortly after, the Court vote in two critical New Deal cases was five to four in favor of the legislation.[51] In *NLRB* v. *Jones and Loughlin Steel Corporation* (1937) and *Steward Machine Company* v. *Davis* (1937), the Supreme Court majority validated the National Labor Relations Act and the Social Security Act. In that same year, it also carefully distinguished but did not overturn *Hammer* when it announced its opinion in *Kentucky Whip and Collar*.

In this environment, the Fair Labor Standards Act was passed. It was an attempt by the Congress to establish a comprehensive scheme of minimum wages and maximum hours for all workers engaged in the production of goods that eventually moved in interstate commerce. The goal was to eliminate substandard labor conditions in some American states. The act fixed minimum wages at twenty-five cents per hour, and maximum hours of weekly employment without overtime (at a required time and one half) were set at forty four hours per week for all workers engaged in the production of goods for interstate commerce. The statue forbade, under pain of six months' imprisonment and/or up to $10,000 fine, violation by employers of such minimum wages and maximum hours; shipment by the employer in interstate commerce of any goods in the process of which any employee was employed in violation of the minimum wage/maximum hour provisions; and failure of the employer to keep records of employee wages and hours.

The lumber industry illustrated the evils that the act was directed at and attempted to resolve. Lumber mills shipped their goods interstate for all but three states in America. In 1933, average hourly wages for the lumber industry were 9.4¢; a weekly salary was but $3.76. In 1938, the year the act was passed, lumber mill operators in Georgia were paying their workers between 12.5¢ and 17¢ per hour.[52] Fred Darby owned a lumber mill in which he processed timber for sale in interstate commerce. He violated the act by refusing to pay minimum wages and required overtime pay as well as by not recording payments of wages to his workers. Indicted in the U.S. district court for paying his workers less and working them more, his lawyers filed a demurrer with the court.

The demurrer challenged the validity of the act under both the commerce clause and the Tenth Amendment, as well as the *Hammer* precedent. The district court judge annulled the indictment in its entirety on the basis of the demurrer, and the government appealed to the Supreme Court.

The government's strategy was simple; the Justice Department would ask the Court to overturn directly the *Hammer* decision. Because of the similarity of facts between the Child Labor Act, which attempted to establish maximum hours for certain workers (children) producing goods for interstate shipment in commerce, and the Fair Labor Standards Act, which established hours and wages requirements and prohibited the movement in interstate commerce of the (innocent and harmless) goods produced by workers employed in violation of the act, the Court could not distinguish *Hammer* any more. If the act was to be validated, *Hammer* had to be confronted and overturned.

It can no longer be asserted that the power of Congress to restrict or condition interstate commerce is limited to articles in themselves harmful or deleterious. . . . The Act, intended to prevent unfair competition and the spread of harmful conditions in interstate commerce, has a goal which is commercial in the strictest sense. But, even if it were concerned simply with humanitarian ends, it would nonetheless be within the commerce power. That power is measured by what it regulates, not by what it affects.[53]

The government argued that the states are incapable of coping with national economic inequities. Employers with lower labor standards possess an unfair labor advantage in interstate competition, and only the national government can deal with the problem. Duplicating the argument of the Justice Department in *Hammer* twenty-two years earlier, the lawyers pointed out that low labor standards were detrimental to the health and efficiency of workers and caused the channels of interstate commerce to spread these unfair labor conditions to other states.

With respect to the argument that the Tenth Amendment was a restraint on the power of Congress to use the Commerce clause, the government argued that the amendment "merely" reserved to the states powers not delegated to the United States. It was not and was never intended to be a limitation upon the exercise of powers delegated to the federal government, concluded the Justice Department argument.

The attorneys for Darby, the appellee in the case, rested their case on the need for preserving the duality of sovereignties under the Constitution. It was, essentially. a dual federalism argument. The act "attempts to regulate conditions in the production of goods, and can not be sustained as a power delegated to Congress to regulate interstate commerce." Prohibiting shipment in interstate commerce was not within the congressional power if the goods themselves are harmless and innocent, they argued, citing as precedent *Hammer* v. *Dagenhart*.

A clear distinction exists between the power of Congress to prohibit interstate shipments of harmful and deleterious goods and its power to regulate shipments of useful commodities. . . . Conditions in production like those involved here have always been held to affect interstate commerce only indirectly. Their control is therefore subject solely to the reserved powers of the states.

With respect to the nature of the federal system, Darby's attorneys, much like Dagenhart's two decades earlier, maintained that to give Congress such an unlimited power would be to destroy the system of dual federalism. If "prohibition *per se* be valid, Congress could deny the channels of interstate commerce to commodities produced with labor of a certain creed or color."

The government's argument is an indirect attack upon the dual system of government established by the Constitution. The Government would solve the problem of the division of governmental powers by rendering the Federal government dominant in all commercial and economic matters. . . . The fact that individual states cannot adequately protect the markets which lie outside their borders for the orderly sale of their products does not vest in the national government unqualified power to regulate competition in those interstate markets.[54]

THE DECISION: MR. JUSTICE STONE

For the Court two principal questions were raised in the litigation as well as the question of what to do with *Hammer v. Dagenhart*. The first question was whether Congress has constitutional power to prohibit in interstate commerce the shipment of lumber manufactured by employees whose wage is less than the prescribed minimum or whose hours are more than the prescribed maximum outlined in the act. The second was whether the Congress has the power to prohibit the employment of workers in the production of goods for interstate commerce at other than prescribed wages and hours.

While conceding that the manufacture or production of goods is itself not commerce, the Court held that "the shipment of manufactured goods interstate is such commerce and the prohibition of such shipment by Congress is indubitably a regulation of the commerce." The power, said Stone, extends to those regulations that aid and foster commerce "but embraces those which prohibit it," citing the earlier cases involving impure foods and so forth that had been distinguished by the Day opinion in *Hammer*.

The "courts are given no control" with respect to matters of legislative judgment, said Stone, again refuting the Day opinion, which looked into purpose and motive of legislation. The power of Congress over interstate commerce is "complete in itself, may be exercised to its utmost extent, and acknowledges no limitations other than are prescribed in the Constitution," wrote the Chief Justice, quoting from John Marshall's opinion in *Gibbons* v. *Ogden*. So long as the Congress has the power to regulate, the motive and purpose of such legislation "are matters for the legislative judgment" alone. Courts have no control and cannot restrict such judgments of the people's representatives unless the act is palpably unconstitutional.

Whatever their motive and purpose, regulations of commerce which do not infringe some constitutional prohibition are within the plenary power conferred on Congress by the Constitution. . . . We conclude that the prohibition of the interstate shipment of goods produced under the forbidden substandard labor conditions is within the constitutional authority of Congress.

The Court then confronted the earlier case of *Hammer* v. *Dagenhart*. *Hammer* "cannot be reconciled with the reasoning and conclusion which we have reached." *Hammer* has not been followed by succeeding courts. Its distinction between harmless and harmful and deleterious products "has long since been abandoned." Its distinction between production and manufacturing "has long since ceased to have force."

The conclusion is inescapable that *Hammer* v. *Dagenhart* was a departure from the principles which have prevailed in the interpretation of the Commerce Clause both before and since the decision and that such vitality, as a precedent, as it then had has long since been exhausted. It should be and now is overruled.[55]

With the overturn accomplished, the Court went to the second question of importance it had raised: the validity of the wage and hour requirement. Elaborating upon the overturn of *Hammer*, which separated intrastate production and manufacturing and other local conditions from the control of the Congress through the commerce clause, the Court argued that so long as these local conditions are related to interstate commerce, they can be brought under the control of Congress. The Fair Labor Standards Act prevented not only the transportation of goods manufactured under substandard labor conditions but also attempted to "stop the initial step toward transportation, production with the purpose of so transporting it."

Such a restriction "on the production of goods for commerce is a permissible exercise of the commerce power." The congressional power extends to intrastate activities "which so affect interstate Commerce . . . as to make regulation of them appropriate means to the attainment of a legitimate end, the exercise of the granted power to regulate interstate commerce." The authority Stone cited was another of Chief Justice Marshall's watershed opinions, *McCulloch* v. *Maryland* (1819), which discussed the importance of the necessary and proper clause in the exercise of powers of the national government. Where purely local activities have a "substantial effect on interstate commerce," they in effect are commerce and subject to the control and prohibition placed upon them by the national legislature.

Stone gave short notice to the Tenth Amendment argument, so important in the *Hammer* decision of the majority and in the argumentation of the Darby lawyers. "Our conclusion," he wrote, "is unaffected by it. . . . The Amendment states but a truism that is all is retained which has not been surrendered." Nothing in the history of the amendment suggests that it was more than "declaratory of the relationship between the national and state governments."

From the beginning and for many years (except for Hammer and other exceptions) the amendment has been construed as not depriving the national government of authority to resort to all means for the exercise of a granted power which are appropriate and plainly adapted to the permitted end.

Thus the Court opinion in *Darby* invalidated the presumptions and conceptions present in *Hammer* so thoroughly that the Court had to invalidate its earlier opinion.

THE IMPACT OF *DARBY*

With the judgment of a unanimous Supreme Court in *Darby*, an age came to an end: the age of economic individualism, laissez-faire, and dual federalism. The Court had said that it would respect any attempt in good faith (consistent with the Constitution) by

Congress to cope with a national problem. There would be judicial review, under proper circumstances, but the Court would not look into the motives and purpose of the congressional statute. If the statute did not violate another clause of the constitution, it was constitutional. Constitutionality was thus separated from the justices' perceptions of what was a wise, good action of the Congress. The impression was left on some that the powers remaining to the states in connection with regulating the products of manufacturing "are those which Congress does not choose to exercise."[56]

Many considered Darby to be an opinion with great doctrinal significance, yet it was not a revolutionary, novel doctrine.[57] It was not novel because the opinion "spoke in the language of McCulloch v. Maryland."[58] Yet it had great doctrinal significance because it put to rest the arguments against national power that had been voiced in *Hammer* and elsewhere: dual federalism; indirect versus direct; harmful versus harmless; and production as opposed to transportation in interstate commerce.[59].

Since the ruling in *Darby*, the Supreme Court has not invalidated an action of Congress based on the commerce clause. In 1968, it sustained extensions to the Fair Labor Standards Act passed in 1961 and 1966 that covered "all employees of any enterprise engaged in the production of goods for commerce" also included employees of hospitals, nursing homes, and educational institutions.[60]

The use of the commerce clause with respect to civil rights and public accommodations, the Civil Rights Act of 1964, was also validated by the Supreme Court in the 1964 cases of *Heart of Atlanta Motel* v. *United States* (1964) and *Katzenbach* v. *McClung* (1964). The use of commerce to achieve social and political goals such as integration of public facilities that are "unrelated to genuine concerns with national commerce"[61] has caused some legal scholars concern, as well as one Supreme Court justice. Justice Douglas, concurring in *Heart of Atlanta* and *Katzenbach,* said" [My reluctance to join with the majority opinion] is not due to any conviction that Congress lacks power to regulate commerce in the interests of human rights. It is rather my belief that the right of the people to be free of state action that discriminates against them because of race, occupies a more protected position in our constitutional system than does the movement of cattle, fruit, steel, and coal across state lines."[62]

In sum, the impact of *Darby* has been significant. It has opened up the commerce clause for use in civil rights, criminal justice,[63] control of agricultural foodstuffs,[64] and just about any other activity that the Congress believes will be in the national interest. The question still to be considered is whether *Darby* was a reasonable, statesmanlike overturn.

THE OVERTURN: CRAFTSMANSHIP OR FIAT?

A reasonable overturn is one that is well thought out, well reasoned, reflects major impersonal reasons for the overturn, and strikes a sensitive balance between the values associated with continuity and those associated with the changing patterns and mores of the society. Rightness, definiteness, and principle were the three basic criteria suggested in chapter 2 when reviewing an overturn opinion of the Supreme Court. Because of the basic fact similarity between the Fair Labor Standards Act of 1938 and the Child Labor Act of 1916, the Supreme Court could either follow *Hammer* (in which case it would be determinative precedent) or, if the Court majority in 1941 believed that *Hammer* was wrongly decided, it could overturn the earlier opinion.[65] It could not distinguish, ignore, or narrow the child labor opinion. It chose to overrule and, on the whole, its overturn opinion was a reasoned one.

RIGHTNESS OF THE OPINION

Was *Hammer* in error with respect to the reality of the economic system? Was it wrong then or was the view of economic reality written in 1918 modified by the changing economic and social realities of the following decades? Did the child labor case follow earlier precedent? Was it a departure from standards of stare decisis? In short, was it a correct judgment?

Hammer v. *Dagenhart* did not "capture the changed social consciousness" of the American society.[66] Permeated with the personal fears and convictions of the five-man majority, it was an error-riddled opinion. It ignored major judicial pronouncements on the question of national power and the extensiveness of the commerce power in particular. In the face of a national economic market that knew no state borders, the Court majority spoke of dual federalism and the ability of individual states to cope with the problems of a twentieth-century industrialism. The opinion of the majority seemed strangely out of place amid the cacophony of business activity in America. It recalled visions of an earlier, frontier America where states could control effectively the forces of production within their borders. But even in 1918, it was a sheer anachronism.

The *Darby* overturn erased the error. It was a necessary and justified erasure. In so annulling the law of the Court, the 1941 opinion returned to basic principles. When it eradicated *Hammer,* the Court affirmed what most legal scholars knew: *Hammer* was a mistake of history, a misreading of the Constitution by five fallible justices. Confronted with the error, the Court frontally attacked and overturned it with appropriate reasons for that dramatic action. Since the clarification of the error in *Darby,* the precedent of *Darby* has been a vital, viable one with respect to economic, social, and political growth and development of the society.

DEFINITENESS OF THE OPINION

Darby brought clarity to the subject of the congressional use of the power to regulate interstate commerce. It removed the confusing and contradictory terms from the legal language (direct versus indirect commercial activities; harmful versus harmless goods; local production versus interstate transportation) that had been part and parcel of *Hammer* v. *Dagenhart.* The Court in 1941 had seen that "progress has knit the country together so that any regulation attempted must operate across state lines to be effective."[67] Until *Hammer* was overturned, it was narrowed, distinguished, and worked around—except for the issue of regulation of a class of labor. Respect for precedent had allowed it to exist so long as its impreciseness and errors did not directly conflict with later Court actions. But in 1941, a unanimous Supreme Court, confronted with a choice between retaining an unclear, erroneous opinion (thereby overturning the Fair Labor Standards Act) and overturning *Hammer,* thereby validating the 1938 act, chose the latter course of action. The 1918 opinion, a divided one condemned by most legal scholars and not followed by the Court in cases that followed *Hammer*, was set aside. *Darby* clearly and definitely established parameters of federal power by removing personal encrustations upon the Constitution that reflected an erroneous view of the federal system.

PRINCIPLE

The overturn decision was not innovation as much as it was a confirmation of principles established two centuries earlier. *Darby* heralded a trend back to principles originally enunciated by John Marshall and others at the 1787 Constitutional Convention; the language of the Constitution by those who wrote the document; and the spirit in which the Constitution was written.[68] What was invalidated by the overturn was the concept of dual federalism. Madison's views, a minority view at the convention, proved to be outmoded ideas in the presence of modern business conditions.[69] (Although Madison was a strong believer in the concept of a balanced government and checks and balances in the form of separation of powers and dual federalism, even he believed that the Congress would be constrained by the political processes, not by the Supreme Court. He disagreed with the view that the national government could suppress state responsibilities in economic matters of local concern but believed that vigorous opposition to such national ventures, in states themselves and in the form of opposition forces in Congress, factions, and so forth would curb the national legislature. In any event, he did not see the Supreme Court's taking an active role in determining the parameters of the powers of the other coordinate branches of the national government.)

Going back to the language of the constitutional convention and the opinions of the early Supreme Court under the leadership of Chief Justice John Marshall, the overturn opinion went to the essence of a principled judgment: justification in accordance with a viable interpretation of the ideal element, the Constitution. The *Darby* view of the commerce clause seemed to be consistent with the intent of the framers; it was consistent with the very basic concept of the Constitution—to form a more perfect union. It did not do injustice to the spirit of the Constitution.

In sum, *Hammer* was a sharply divided, poorly written decision of the Supreme Court. It was not, except for the issue of child labor, viable precedent. It was not supported by legal authorities, who saw it as a personal statement of judicial discontent with the events and crises of modern society. It was not supported by later Court opinions. It was, in effect, a judicial orphan, deserted by its progeny. It reflected a philosophy of government that was not acceptable at the time the document was written; it reflected an attitude of a judicial body that was repugnant to the men who wrote the document. It was erroneous, unclear, and inconsistent with the basic principles of the Constitution and the intent of its framers.

A good overturn does not abandon the vision of the founding fathers. *Darby*, with its insistence on fundamental constitutional government, returned the commerce clause to where it was before *Hammer* was decided. In effect, *Hammer* was a detour in the history of the commerce clause; *Darby* repaired the road and cleared the channels of interstate commerce. Darby linked the past with the present and future; *Gibbons* v. *Ogden* was linked with *Wickard* and *Wirtz* and *Katzenbach*. *Darby* not only was the repaired road; it was the constitutional bridge between past principles of government and present and future social and economic problems that had to be dealt with by the national government.

SUMMARY

This chapter has focused on an overturn by a Supreme Court that reflected the New Deal attitude of President Franklin Roosevelt. Five of the justices had been appointed by Roosevelt after the court packing plan was introduced in 1937: Stanley Reed, Hugo Black, Felix Frankfurter, William Douglas, and Frank Murphy. (Chief Justice Stone was elevated to that position by Roosevelt.) Yet the opinion overturning *Hammer* v. *Dagenhart* was relatively free of the personal, ideological element that was so apparent in the *Hammer* opinion. It was a well reasoned, well-thought-out opinion, combining political statesmanship with judicial deference to the popularly elected branches of government.

If the child labor case was faulty, erroneous, inconsistent with past principle, and poor precedent, *Darby* was the opposite. The

1941 overturn opinion, principled and reasoned, has continued to be viable, energetic precedent over three decades later. It reflected the vision of the framers; it bridged the gap between revered past and troubled present and future.

NOTES

1. Thomas R. Powell, "The Child Labor Law, the Tenth Amendment and the Commerce Clause," *Southern Law Quarterly* 3 (August 1918): 189.

2. See, generally, C. B. Swisher, *American Constitutional Development* (Boston: Little, Brown 1954), pp. 24-5.

3. Henry W. Bickle, "The Commerce Power and Hammer v. Dagenhart," *University of Pennsylvania Law Review* 67 (1919): 32.

4. Robert L. Stern, "The Commerce Clause and the National Economy," *Harvard Law Review* 59 (May-July 1946): 947; see also Robert Stern, "That Commerce Concerns More States Than One," *Harvard Law Review* 47 (1934): 1337-1338.

5. Stern, "That Commerce," pp. 1337-1338.

6. *Gibbons* v. *Ogden*, 22 U.S.1 (1824). See also Stern, *op. cit.*, "Developments in the Use of the Commerce Clause as a Basis for Federal Economic Regulation," *Minnesota Law Review* 24 (1940): 941.

7. Edward S. Corwin, "Congress's Power to Prohibit Commerce: A Crucial Constitutional Issue," *Cornell Law Quarterly* 18 (June 1933): 485.

8. See, generally, ibid.

9. Ibid., p. 488.

10. Ibid.

11. "The commerce clause was intended as a negative and preventive provision against injustice in the states themselves, rather than as a power to be used for the positive purposes of the general government." James Madison in Max Farrand, ed., *The Records of the Federal Constitutional Convention of 1787* (New Haven: Yale University Press, 1911), p. 268.

12. *Champion* v. *Ames*, 88 U.S. 321 (1903).

13. Ibid.

14. *E. C. Knight* was "literalism run riot, for no commerce in manufacturing is not found in the Constitution, but was invented by a court. It has not stood, but before it passed from the picture, it produced an heir in *Hammer* v. *Dagenhart*." J. A. C. Grant, "Commerce, Production, and the Fiscal Powers of Congress, *Yale Law Journal* 45 (March 1936): 753.

15. Bickle, op. cit., p. 28.

16. *United States* v. *Popper*, 98 F. Supp 423 (1899).

17. *Hoke* v. *United States,* 227 U.S. 308 (1913).

18. *Hipolite Egg Company* v. *United States,* 220 U.S. 45 (1911).

19. Ibid.

20. Animal Husbandries Act, 1910.

21. *Clark Distilling Company* v. *Western Maryland Railroad Co.,* 242 U.S. 311 (1917).

22. Robert Cushman, "The National Police Power Under the Commerce Clause of the Constitution," *Minnesota Law Review* 3 (1919): 381–412.

23. Appellants' brief, *Hammer* v. *Dagenhart,* p. 254.

24. See *Hammer,* 268-269, for Child Labor Act.

25. Ibid., 252–259.

26. Ibid., 260–268.

27. Andrew Bruce, "Interstate Commerce and Child Labor," *Minnesota Law Review* 3 (1918): 90–91.

28. Ibid., p. 89.

29. "Commerce Clause," *New York University Law Review* 18 (1941): 577–578.

30. "Interstate Commerce and National Powers," *Missouri Law Review* 6 (1941): 362.

31. Bickle, op. cit., p. 29; Powell, op. cit., p. 202.

32. Powell, op. cit., pp. 182–183.

33. Corwin, op. cit., p. 502.

34. Ibid., p. 503.

35. Grant, op. cit., p. 754.

36. Powell, op. cit., pp. 185–186.

37. "Commerce Clause," p. 578.

38. Thomas R. Powell, "Child Labor, Congress, and the Constitution," *North Carolina Law Review* 1 (November 1922): 64–65.

39. Powell, "Child Labor Law," p. 189.

40. "Commerce Clause," p. 577.

41. Powell, "Child Labor Law," p. 177.

42. "Interstate Commerce," *University of Pennsylvania Law Review* 89 (1941): 820.

43. Ibid.

44. "Interstate Commerce," *Washington and Lee Law Review* 2 (1941): 284.

45. "Constitutionality of the Fair Labor Standards Act," *Illinois Law Review* 35 (1941): 876.

46. *Kentucky Whip and Collar Company* v. *Illinois Central Railroad Company,* 299 U.S. 334 (1937).

47. Note, "Child Labor Law," p. 876.

48. Stern, "Commerce Clause," p. 944.

49. Ibid; see also John Farage, "That which 'Directly' Affects Commerce," *Dickinson Law Review* 42 (1937): 1.

50. *Carter* v. *Carter Coal Company*, 298 U.S. 238 (1935); *United States* v. *Butler*, 297 U.S. 1 (1936); *Schecter Poultry Company* v. *United States*, 295 U.S. 495 (1935); *Railroad Retirement Board* v. *Alton Railroad*, 295 U.S. 330 (1935); *Louisville Joint Stock Company* v. *Radford*, 295 U.S. 555 (1935); *Ashton* v. *Cameron County District*, 298 U.S. 513 (1936).

51. See, generally, Robert H. Jackson, *The Struggle for Judicial Supremacy* (New York: Alfred A. Knopf, Inc., 1941).

52. Stern, "Commerce Clause," p. 886.

53. Ibid.

54. Ibid., p. 888.

55. Appellants' brief, at 117.

56. "Interstate Commerce," *Loyola Law Review* 1 (1941): 101.

57. Stern, "Commerce Clause," pp. 946–947.

58. Ibid.

59. Ibid.

60. *Maryland* v. *Wirtz*, 392 U.S. 183 (1968). But see *National League of Cities* v. *Usury*, 96 SCT 2465 (1976).

61. See for example, William B. Lockhart et al., *The American Constitution* (St. Paul: West Publishing Company, 1975), p. 133.

62. *Katzenbach* v. *McClung* 379 U.S. 294 (1964).

63. *Perez* v. *United States*, 402 U.S. 146 (1971).

64. *Wickard* v. *Filburn*, 317 U.S. 111 (1942).

65. "Commerce Clause," p. 577.

66. "Interstate Commerce," p. 283.

67. "Interstate Commerce and National Powers," p. 363.

68. Stern, "Commerce Clause," p. 947.

69. Corwin, op, cit., p. 504

4 The Flag Salute Cases

The First Amendment to the United States Constitution contains the basic substantive rights Americans possess that protect them from governmental oppression. This chapter will examine a handful of Supreme Court decisions dealing with the freedom of religion which is protected by the First Amendment: "Congress shall make no law respecting an establishment of religion, or prohibiting the free exercise thereof." The problem for the Supreme Court was to define the meaning of free exercise of religion.

In the 1940 decision in *Cantwell* v. *Connecticut*, Justice Reed for the Court said that freedom of religion "embraces two concepts: freedom to believe and freedom to act. The first is absolute but in the nature of things the second cannot be. Conduct remains subject to regulation for the protection of society."[1] It is essentially the conflicts surrounding the second concept, conduct, that have caused the greatest controversy. The conflict arises when a state or local community enacts legislation for the good of the community's morals, safety, health, or welfare and whose purpose is essentially nonreligious. However, that legislation may either prohibit or excessively burden the conduct of groups dictated by their religious beliefs or require conduct that the religious group is forbidden to engage in because of their religious beliefs.

In the resolution of this controversy courts and judges have had to balance the rights of the individual and the rights of the society to maintain order for the public welfare. The cases discussed in this chapter involve state and local ordinances that compelled members of a religious sect, the Jehovah's Witnesses, to salute the flag of

America in school. For the members of this group, this conduct was prohibited by their religious beliefs, and they defied the statutes. This controversial issue came to the Supreme Court during its October 1939 term.

RELIGIOUS FREEDOM AND THE JEHOVAH'S WITNESSES TO *GOBITIS*, 1940

The Jehovah's Witnesses sect, described by one legal scholar as a religious group that is a "mixture of several ancient heresies, touch of fundamentalism, first century echatology, pacificism . . .a simple fanaticism," in less than three decades brought eighty-seven cases to the Supreme Court.[2] It won all but twelve, and some of those it lost were subsequently overturned by later Court majorities. Chief Justice Stone once said of the sect: "They ought to have an endowment in view of the aid they give in solving the legal problems of civil liberties."[3]

The group challenged local ordinances that: required license taxes for solicitors, restricted marching in the streets, and prohibited canvassing, the use of loudspeakers, the use of children when distributing literature, the use of blasphemous, obscene, or "fighting words" on the public streets, soliciting in company towns, and so on. They argued that these ordinances restricted their religious freedom. "Probably the most celebrated was the flag salute cases, *Gobitis* and *Barnette*."[4]

Prior to the litigation of the Witnesses, which began in 1937, many statutes had been validated because they prohibited certain practices, considered religious by some, thought to be a reasonable danger to the public health, safety, morals, and welfare. Polygamy, refusal to take the oath of allegiance to defend the nation, free use of sacramental wine, refusal to be vaccinated, use of obscene language, blasphemy, dissemination of lewd literature, refusal of a prospective groom to undergo required physical examination, faith healing without medical qualifications, parading and beating of drums, practicing medicine without a license, disrespect for the Sabbath, and the handling of poisonous snakes are some acts validated by the Supreme Court that conflicted with the religious conduct of certain sects.[5] The Witnesses found these and other ordinances to be contrary to the freedom of religious expression they had in the Constitution, but the ordinances they considered most obnoxious were the flag salute statutes. They found these laws "most offensive, demanding that school children salute the flag, for that application is felt by most of their families."[6]

The flag salute began in America in 1892 as a "fitting gesture in the commemoration of the four hundredth anniversary of the landing of Columbus."[7] The National Education Association in that year resolved to continue the anniversary celebration in all possible ways and proceeded to sponsor the adoption of the flag salute and pledge of allegiance in all the public schools throughout the country. Kansas was the first state to adopt the salute into law in 1907 and, during World War I, most states developed similar statutes. The law soon became compulsory but was never challenged in court until 1937.[8] The laws varied about how to punish violators of the flag salute statute. Some were silent on penalties; others punished parents; still others expelled children; and others treated children who were expelled as delinquent and raised the specter of banishment to reformatory for not saluting the flag. The flag salute statutes were written by state as well as local legislators; some compelled all public school children to salute the flag while others required students in all schools, public and private, to salute the flag.

The Jehovah's Witnesses were opposed to the flag salute on religious grounds because of their views of Exodus 20:1-6: "Thou shalt have no other gods before me; Thou shalt not make unto thee any graven image, or any likeness of any thing that is in heaven above, or that is in the earth beneath, or that is in the water under the earth; thou shalt not bow down thyself to them, nor serve them." Saluting the flag, perhaps an innocent gesture for Jews and Catholics, was for the Witnesses bowing down to idols.

At the time of *Minersville* v. *Gobitis,* a case coming to the Supreme Court from Pennsylvania, eighteen states had compulsory flag salute laws, and the Witnesses had initiated suits in twelve of these states.[9] Five were brought against the parents for their children's refusal to salute; five were brought against the children for being "habitual delinquents." In most of the cases, the courts refused to send the children to reform school or to fine the parents, but the judges also refused to compel reinstatement of the pupils who were expelled from school for refusal to salute the flag. The options facing the Witness parents were: public school and the compulsory flag salute, private schools (which were costly) or the possibility of fine or imprisonment or, minimally, nothing at all (the child was expelled, not punished, but not allowed to reenter until he or she saluted the flag).

The Supreme Court had not chosen to hear any of the cases on the merits. It dismissed Massachusetts, Georgia, and New Jersey court decisions "for want of a substantial federal question."[10] Until *Gobitis*, then, state courts were in a quandary with respect to the issue of flag salutes and religious freedom arguments. They could not compel children to salute; neither would they punish them or their parents for nonrefusal. They could not order school boards to reinstate or excuse them from the flag ceremony. It was a "stalemated issue."[11]

In this stalemate, two themes emerged from the state cases that were to be important questions for the Supreme Court justices. The first was that the flag salute had nothing at all to do with religion; the judges decided that there was no question of freedom of religious expression posed in the flag salute dispute. An important corollary to this problem is whether the state should make this judgment or whether this is a matter for the individual to decide. This question was discussed by the Supreme Court in both *Gobitis* and the overturn of *Gobitis*, *West Virginia Board of Education* v. *Barnette* (1943). A second question was the position taken by some judges that the salute laws are a justifiable exercise of the state police power; that is, in the interest of patriotism and national unity, the state is justified in compelling the flag salute.

THE FIRST FLAG SALUTE CASE; *MINERSVILLE V. GOBITIS* (1940)

FACTS AND CONSTITUTIONAL ISSUES

Lillian, age twelve, and her brother William Gobitis, age ten, were expelled from the public school of the small town of Minersville, Pennsylvania. The local board of education had required both teachers and children to salute the national flag in school every day. Because Pennsylvania law made school attendance compulsory, the Gobitis parents had to send their two children to private school. The Gobitis's were Jehovah's Witnesses, and the salute to the flag was, to them, an act that contravened the Bible. Because of the financial burden thus placed on the family, the parents sought to enjoin the authorities from continuing to exact participation in the flag salute controversy as a condition of their children's attendances at the Minersville public school.

In U.S. Federal District Court Judge Ralph Maris, Gobitis found brief respite. After reviewing the earlier state cases that had been affirmed without review by the Supreme Court, Maris noted that the judges in these cases had not discerned the fundamental principle that no one—whether school educator or judge—has the right to censor another's religious convictions unless compelled to do so by an overriding public necessity:

No man is empowered to set bounds to the areas of human conduct in which these convictions should be permitted to control his actions, unless compelled to do so by an overriding public necessity which properly requires the exercise of the police power.
It seems obvious that their refusal to salute the flag could not in any way prejudice or imperil the public safety, health, or morals or the property or personal rights of their fellow citizens.[12]

The view of the judge was that, absent a clear and present danger to the community from the children's refusal to salute a flag, there was no legislative power to compel them to so act. This judgment was affirmed by the Third Circuit Court of Appeals, and Gobitis thus became the only flag salute case where the lower federal courts invalidated the salute statute. The Minersville school board then appealed to the United States Supreme Court, which for the first time in this controversy, granted certiorari and ordered full arguments on the subject. The Court probably granted the writ because the lower courts had decided contrary to earlier Supreme Court per curiam opinions that, in effect, had upheld court judgments validating flag salute statutes in New Jersey, New York, Massachusetts, and Georgia.[13]

Before the Supreme Court, the lawyers for the school board made two fundamental arguments. First, the state had the power and authority to expel children from school who disobeyed basic, general requirements of school attendance. The flag salute was one such general requirement, and it did not violate any personal right under the Pennsylvania constitution and the U.S. Constitution. A second argument made was that, in the state's judgment, the refusal to salute the flag by the Gobitis children was not founded on a religious belief. Instead, the salute was simply one of many ways in which a citizen showed respect for the government.

The act of saluting a flag has no bearing on what a pupil may think of his creator or what are his relations to his creator. Nor is a pupil required to exhibit his religious sentiments in a particular "form of worship" when saluting the flag, because the ceremony is not, by any stretch of the imagination, a "form of worship." Like the study of history or civics or the doing of any other act which might make a pupil more patriotic or teach him or her "loyalty to the State and National Government," the salute has no religious implications.[14]

In sum, the board's argument was that there was no religious significance attached to the flag salute. As such, the personal liberty argument was irrelevant because no personal liberties were being infringed upon by such a patriotic act. Therefore the state had the power to enforce penalties associated with the refusal to salute in school.

The attorneys for the respondents, the Gobitis children and their parents, made three basic points. First they argued, echoing Judge Maris's views, that the children's rights of conscience were violated by the law: "Shall man be free to exercise his conscientious belief in God and his obedience to God's commands in law, or shall man be compelled to obey a state law that is in direct conflict with the law of God?" The individual alone is privileged to determine what to believe. The school board was telling the children what they ought to believe; the law coerced and compelled the children to violate their religious beliefs and therefore the statute was null and void.

The second query raised before the Supreme Court was whether a court or a legislature can say whether the Witnesses mistakenly interpreted Exodus. The point was that the Gobitis's belief was based on the Bible. They believed that saluting the flag is a form of religious activity that constitutes idolatry. The First Amendment's freedom of religious expression gives them this right to believe and to interpret the Bible as they wish. A state law that prohibits their belief and, worse, compels them to act contrary to their belief is unconstitutional.

Finally the attorneys pointed out that the flag salute was a new experiment and not a practice that had been established when the country was formed. To expel students from schools and deny them the opportunity of a public education because they refused to violate their conscience in carrying out an educational experiment (in learning patriotism by the constant saluting of the flag) was wrong and a cruel and unusual punishment.[15]

The arguments came down to the freedom of religious conscience versus the development of national unity through a compulsory flag salute (liberty versus state authority). The justices of the Supreme Court were thus confronted with a fundamental dilemma: weighing and balancing competing values that were part of the ideal element of law, the Constitution of the United States.

THE OPINIONS

THE MAJORITY OPINION: MR. JUSTICE FRANKFURTER

The majority was aware of the severe nature of the controversy: the conflict between liberty of conscience and the need to safeguard the "nation's fellowship." The "crucial question" the Court had to answer was "whether the requirement of participation in such a flag salute ceremony, exacted from a child who refuses upon sincere religious grounds, infringes without due process of law the religious liberty guaranteed [by the First Amendment through] the Fourteenth Amendment." (The Court majority accepted the fact that the refusal to salute was a "sincere religious belief.")

Government could interfere with religious expression if the general legislation was not directed at the doctrinal loyalties of particular religious sects. The secular interests of the majority in the community often clash with the views of small sects in the larger community. The question Frankfurter raised was, "When does the Constitutional guarantee compel exemption from doing what society thinks necessary for the promotion of some great, common end, or from a penalty for conduct which appears dangerous to the public good?"[16]

The majority was saying that even though the religious conviction might be sincere, in the interest of some "great national end," the state could compel religious believers to set aside their religious convictions or go to jail on their behalf. Frankfurter was also suggesting that the refusal to salute the flag, religious though it might be, might very well be "dangerous" conduct.

"Conscientious scruples," Frankfurter wrote, "have not, in the long struggle for religious toleration, relieved the individual from obedience to a general law not aimed at the promotion or restriction of religious beliefs." In a democracy, all citizens have political responsibilities that must be performed regardless of sincerely held religious convictions. These responsibilities were essential, the Court reasoned, "for the orderly, tranquil, and free society without which religious toleration itself is unattainable."[17] (In effect, the majority was telling the Witnesses that losing liberty now was essential to the retention of religious toleration later on.)

The goal of the flag salute law was to promote national cohesion, an interest "inferior to none in the hierarchy of legal values. National unity is the basis of national security." To prevent the government from selecting appropriate means to achieve this end is to endanger the national existence, the Court reasoned. No democratic government, maintained Frankfurter (quoting President Lincoln), must be too weak to maintain its own life. If governmental leaders believe that in order to foster the "binding ties of cohesive sentiment," the symbols of the society, a flag salute (the flag being the symbol of national unity) is necessary, then judges must not substitute their personal notions for those of the legislators and other political forces to invalidate such judgments.[18]

Courts, especially the Supreme Court, possessed no marked and certainly no controlling pedagogical competence. They should not make educational policies for the society. The legislature, stated the majority, was not barred from choosing appropriate means to reach the desired end of national cohesiveness and unity, without which there cannot be any liberties, civil or religious. If the end was legitimate, though the means be still "uncertain and unauthenticated," or even "folly," then the means are not unconstitutional. In any event, the courtroom is not the proper arena for debating such issues of policy. "To hold otherwise would in effect make us the school board for the country."[19]

If there is merit in the Jehovah's Witnesses' argument (and the Court had earlier admitted the merits), then the political arena not the courtroom, should be the place where debates should take place and changes in the law should be suggested and made. "Personal freedom is best maintained when it is ingrained in the people's habits—so long as the remedial channels of the democratic process remain open and unobstructed—and not enforced against *popular policy* by the coercion of adjudicated law."[20]

The majority reaffirmed the view that society, in the name of self-protection, could use the educational process for inculcating loyalty "even if it means depriving a small minority in the society one of its basic values." In a classic statement of judicial restraint, Frankfurter then stated:

Where all the effective means of inducing political changes are left free from interference, education in the abandonment of foolish legislation is itself a training in liberty. To fight out the wise use of legislative authority in the forum of public opinion and before legislative assemblies rather than to transfer such a contest to the judicial arena, serves to vindicate the self confidence of a free people.[21]

In sum, although the majority saw the serious nature of the conflict between liberty and authority, given the limited role of the Court in the democratic processes the solution to the conflict was to be found, if at all, by the Jehovah's Witnesses' taking their arguments to the arena of public opinion and convincing legislators that the legislation was foolish. For the Supreme Court to enter the controversy would be judicial usurpation of the educational function, and courts were not in that business. The majority refused to be dragged into the swirling controversy surrounding the Witnesses and flag salutes.

The Dissenting Opinion: Mr. Justice Stone

Harlan Fiske Stone was the lone dissenter in *Gobitis* (Justice McReynolds concurred without writing an opinion). In the past, Justice Stone had been highly critical of the majority view that suggested that small political or religious minorities such as the Witnesses could affect policy changes in the larger community by searing the conscience of these more conventional legislators and their constituents. In a famous footnote to a 1938 decision of the Court in *United States* v. *Carolene Products,* Stone had suggested that legislation that restricted First Amendment freedoms should be subjected to more exacting scrutiny then other types of legislation. Careful scrutiny should also be made of statutes that affect particular religious minorities: "Prejudice against discrete and insular minorities may be a special condition, which tends seriously to curtail the operation of those political processes ordinarily to be relied upon to protect minorities, and which may call for a correspondingly more searching judicial inquiry."

Stone's position in *Carolene* was the basis of his dissent in *Gobitis.* Whereas Frankfurter's argument stressed that the Witnesses should go to the political processes for redress of their grievances, Stone suggested that these processes would be closed to the Witnesses. Under such circumstances, the Court had a constitutional responsibility to listen carefully to the Witnesses and scrutinize the legislation with an eye toward the primacy of the First Amendment values.

The law the majority sustained was unique. It did more than prohibit religious activity; it "seeks to coerce these children to express a sentiment which they do not entertain, and which violates their deepest religious convictions." The majority opinion admitted this reality. However, although Stone admitted that constitutional guarantees of liberty were not absolutes and that government, to survive, could deprive citizens of some liberty for the duration of the crisis, this situation was "a long step, and one which I am unable to take, to the position that a government may, as a supposed educational measure and a means of disciplining the young, compel public affirmations which violate their religious conscience."[22]

Short of a clear and present danger to the national existence, the First Amendment freedoms are a barrier to state action. "It is the function of the Courts to determine" the issues and resolve the conflict between liberty and order consistent with the values inherent in the Bill of Rights. Stone asserted that there were ways to teach loyalty and patriotism other "than by compelling the pupil to affirm that which he does not believe and by commanding a form of affirmance which violates his religious convictions."

He concluded by pointing out that "the very essence of liberty for the individual is freedom from compulsion as to what he shall think and what he shall say."

The very terms of the Bill of Rights preclude, it seems to me, any reconciliation of such compulsions with the constitutional guaranties by a legislative declaration that they are more important to the public welfare than the Bill of Rights.[23]

Courts, especially the Supreme Court, ought not to equivocate on such a matter of principle; they should not defer to the political processes the resolution of a constitutional controversy raised by a small minority. Judicial inaction, concluded Stone, "seems to me no less a crime than the surrender of the constitutional protection of the liberty of small minorities to the popular will." The Court must examine such legislative policies with a view toward protecting the individual's civil and religious liberties.

I am not prepared to say (after scrutinizing the legislation in question) that the right of this small and helpless minority, including children having a strong religious conviction, . . . is to be overborne by the interest of the state in maintaining discipline in the schools.[24]

In opposition to his brethren on the bench, Justice Stone insisted upon judicial action rather than leaving the constitutional question to the political processes, which have never been receptive to small, powerless, radical minority opinions throughout American history. The Stone dissent was antithetical to Frankfurter's opinion, both in tone and perspective. It emphasized the primary importance in the scheme of values of the First Amendment, in particular, the importance of freedom of conscience. Justice Stone, however, was a minority of one in *Gobitis*.

EVALUATION AND IMPACT

EVALUATION

The *Gobitis* decision must be viewed in light of the worldwide events of the time. In the spring of 1940, the time of the *Gobitis* announcement, the fear in America of a subversive fifth column "assumed almost hysterical proportions."[25] Jehovah's Witnesses were attacked in some small towns as Nazi agents. In June 1940, the

Gallup poll indicated that 65 percent of the American public believed that Germany would attack America—and that Germany would win the war.[26]

In this atmosphere of impending danger and attack by Germany, the nation became flag conscious. Stores in large cities sold out their stock of flags. "The country was in the grip of war hysteria," bemoaned the liberal *New Republic* in June 1940. In this atmosphere—Nazi armies streaking across the low countries and France, Americans concerned about the possibility of fighting Germany and losing, Jehovah's Witnesses seen as potential spies—the Supreme Court justices heard arguments and decided the constitutional arguments. There had to have been environmental impact on the thinking of the justices; certainly the majority's uncritical acceptance of the national unity argument was a reflection of the Court's awareness of the events taking place in America and in the world.

The vaguely defined term *national unity* was uncritically accepted by the Supreme Court majority as a legitimate end—indeed the most important end—of government and any means justifies that end. The majority opinion did not seek to reconcile the *Gobitis* opinion with earlier liberal Court opinions dealing with civil liberties and religious expression. It distinguished *Gobitis* from *Myer, Society of Sisters, Schneider, Herndon, Hague, De Jonge,* and *Cantwell*[27] (the last decided barely two weeks earlier) because national unity and national existence was far superior to the interests protected in the other cases (canvassing, picketing, protest marches, right of private schools to function, and so forth).[28]

Furthermore the task of determining appropriate means for promoting national unity and patriotism was a legislative matter not subject to judicial scrutiny, argued Frankfurter. The majority opinion did not state whether the salute was a religious rite and whether it was a violation of religious freedoms if it was. The theory propounded was that national unity demanded sacrifices, including religious convictions of small sects, in order for the society to do battle against the impending invader. The Court, in the name of the superior national goal of national unity, "turned its face away from a proper recognition of personal freedoms guaranteed by the Constitution."[29]

The reasoning of the Frankfurter opinion was simple: the state has the power to pass legislation for its own self-preservation; the actions of the Gobitis children fall within the parameters of the state statute; therefore, they are guilty regardless of their own protestations that they were denied freedom of religious belief. Above and beyond the police powers of the state to protect the health, safety, welfare, and well-being of its citizens, the state could legislate in order to promote morale and patriotism.

Accepting the goal of national unity meant that the Court believed that love of country would result from such a forced flag salute ceremony. A consequence of the flag salute accepted begrudgingly by Justice Frankfurter was a growing love of country. But, as the critics of the opinion retorted, "love of democracy grows from within; nurtured only by clean air and the warm sunlight of liberty."[30] Compulsion was not the way to develop patriotism. When a person is forced to violate deeply held convictions, he or she does not develop an increased loyalty; just the opposite occurs.[31] "Patriotism comes from the heart and cannot be inspired nor fostered by compulsion," wrote another critic of the majority opinion in *Gobitis*.

There was deference even though the Court majority confessed that the means to the end might be "folly." The opinion was an expression of a view of the function of the judiciary in a democratic society held by Justice Felix Frankfurter that minimized dramatically the role of the courts in political processes and political controversies. Frankfurter maintained that the Court was an oligarchic institution in a majoritarian democracy; that the only power the judiciary had was moral persuasion; and that the Court was powerless to persuade excited majorities and so should not get involved in what he later called the "political thicket."[32] According to Frankfurter, if the flag salute as a means to the goal of national loyalty was folly, then the legislators had to recognize it as such and change the law. That was the essence of democracy: "training in liberty."

There was no close scrutiny of the impact of the statute because the Court was not a school board; neither was there any attempt to employ a doctrine developed by Justice Oliver W. Holmes in earlier civil liberty cases—clear and present danger. Was there a clear and present danger to the national or local community if the children politely, respectfully refused to salute the American flag? No, not according to the critics of the Court decision. There was no actual showing of a danger to the state in the record, but this argument was rejected by the majority (it was not even mentioned by Justice Frankfurter). When the subject is national unity, clear and present danger is not the standard to be employed in measuring the means used in attaining that goal. More importantly, no test was relevant for the majority because it refused to accept any limitation on state action in the name of national unity and security.[33]

The majority was concerned with the symbols of national unity, not the basic values of the nation. Confronted by the Nazi menace, the Court announced *Gobitis*. It was a decision made "under the influence of an upsurge of popular patriotism."[34] The Court, swayed by popular emotions and prejudices of Americans against any group that seemed different, ignored the constitutional guarantees that were the foundation of the democracy.[35]

If the flag was considered the emblem of freedom, the majority's logic is strained by including in that term an involuntary salute of a schoolboy, fearful of being damned by his Creator for bowing down to what he erroneously but sincerely believes is a graven image.[36]

The reaction to *Gobitis* was almost uniformly critical. Law reviews were violent in their condemnation of the majority opinion; all but three in the country opposed the decision of the Court.[37] Known legal giants such as Zachariah Chafee, Edward Corwin, Robert Cushman, Beryl Levy, Benjamin Wright and John Wilkenson condemned the judgment, labeling it a "backwash" caused by the crisis fervor "produced by the successful march of the Nazi army through France."[38]

The press was also critical of the judgment of the Court. Newspapers in Baltimore, Atlanta, Birmingham, Boston, Chicago, Cincinnati, Columbus, Cleveland, Dallas, Des Moines, Detroit, Fort Worth, Hartford, Louisville, Los Angeles, Memphis, New York, Pittsburgh, Seattle, and other large cities condemned the decision. The *St. Louis Post-Dispatch* reflected their views in its editorial:

The Court is Dead Wrong. Its decision is a violation of American principles. We think it is a surrender to popular hysteria. If patriotism depends on such things as this—on violation of the fundamental right of religious freedom, then it becomes not a noble emotion of love but something to be rammed down our throats by the law. We honor Justice Stone, who refused to lend himself to it.[39]

The press, the legal profession, and the newsweeklies were all opposed to *Gobitis*.[40] But the reality of the political processes in America in 1940 meant that "patrioteers" in rual and small-town America took the opinion as the right to compel adults and children to salute the flag. In America until very recently, small towns like these held political power in the state legislatures. And it was in these small towns that the Jehovah's Witnesses concentrated their religious activities.[41] Frankfurter's opinion meant that these small rural towns could oppress the Witnesses. Frankfurter's mechanistic view of democratic processes, called majoritarian absolutism by a legal critic, meant that if the Witnesses did not convince powerful pressure groups in rural America and thereby induce political change, they would lose their liberties.[42]

In sum, given the war fever and the judicial self-restraint of the Court majority, especially Frankfurter's self-abnegation philosophy of judicial behavior, the Court majority avoided a careful, full discussion of the constitutional issues.

THE IMPACT

Although there were some excessive actions by small towns after *Gobitis*, within months of the decisions the incidents peaked and then died down. The flag salute statute was valid, and the Witnesses had to cope with that fact. They had other confrontations with local governments. One with the towns of Opelika, Alabama, Fort Smith, Arkansas, and Casa Grande, Arizona, led to an action of the Supreme Court "unprecedented in the annals of Supreme Court history."[43]

In the three cases, consolidated into one, *Jones* v. *Opelika*, the Jehovah's Witnesses challenged the common practice of local communities' requiring sellers on the public streets to obtain a license and pay a substantial tax (ten to twenty-five dollars a year) in order to use the streets. Most of the time, the ordinances were general and nondiscriminatory,   but   they   forced   the   religious,   itinerant ministers of the Jehovah's Witnesses sect to pay a fee in order to prosyletize. Almost two years to the day *Gobitis* was announced, the Supreme Court, in a split five-to-four opinion announced its decision in *Opelika*.[44] Indulging in the same presumption that existed in *Gobitis*, the Reed opinion for the majority held that the imposition of the license tax was valid. If the tax is to be changed, urged Reed, the community is the place for the change to be made, not the courts. In any event it was not an unconstitutional ordinance because it was general and nondiscriminatory. The sales of Jehovah's Witnessess pamphlets were commercial and religious at the same time, and the state could tax such sales through the license tax arrangement.[45]

The four dissenters were Chief Justice Stone, the sole dissenter in *Gobitis*, and Justices Black, Douglas, and Murphy, all of whom had joined the Frankfurter opinion in *Gobitis*. Stone and Murphy wrote stinging dissents, pointing out that the statutes violated religious freedom on its face, were a callous disregard of constitutional rights, and that the public streets have always been viewed in America as proper places for dissemination of information without the payment of license taxes. "These heavy taxes prohibit or seriously hinder the distribution of the Jehovah's Witnesses religious literature."[46] Pamphleteering has always been an important part of the American political heritage. Justice Murphy pointed out, and such a prohibitive tax stills the pamphleteer, thus violating constitutionally protected rights.[47]

What was unprecedented in *Opelika* was the public recanting of Justices Black, Douglas, and Murphy. In a separate dissenting opinion they publicly admitted, for the first time in Supreme Court history, that a decision that they had participated in and voted with the majority was wrongly decided. They had denounced an opinion in an otherwise unrelated case and in so doing gave the Jehovah's Witnesses renewed hope in their struggle against the flag salute statute.

The opinion of the Court [in *Opelika*] sanctions a device which in our opinion suppresses or tends to suppress the free exercise of a religion practiced by a minority group. This is but another step in the direction which *Minersville* v *Gobitis* took against the same religious minority and is a logical extension of the principles upon which that decision rested. Since we joined in the opinion in the *Gobitis* case, we think this is an appropriate occasion to state that we now believe that it also was wrongly decided. Our democratic form of government *functioning under* the Bill of Rights has a high responsibility to accommodate itself to religious minorities however unpopular and unorthodox those views may be. The First Amendment does not put the right freely to exercise religion in a *subordinate* position. We fear, however, that the opinions in these and in the *Gobitis* case do exactly that.[48]

The impact of this statement meant that there were at least four votes in favor of overturning *Gobitis*. It also meant that lower federal court judges could expect renewed litigation with respect to the issue of flag salute statutes. The Jehovah's Witnesses went to federal court in West Virginia challenging the state flag salute statute, which had been law since *Gobitis*. All schools in the state—public, private, and denominational—were required to have a flag salute every day. The three-man district court issued an injunction restraining the school board from implementing its expulsion penalty. Judge John Parker, sitting with the Southern District, West Virginia, Federal District Court, said the following in issuing the injunction: "Developments with respect to the Gobitis decision are such that we do not feel that it is incumbent upon us to accept *Gobitis* as guiding authority."[49]

The public admittance of error of the three justices had an obvious impact on the status of *Gobitis* as precedent. Shortly after the district court opinion was announced, the school board appealed the injunction to the Supreme Court and, in 1943, *West Virginia Board of Education* v. *Barnette* was argued before the Court.

THE OVERTURN OF *GOBITIS: WEST VIRGINIA* V. *BARNETTE* (1943)

FACTS AND CONSTITUTIONAL ISSUES

Shortly after the Supreme Court judgment in *Gobitis*, West Virginia amended its statutes to require all schools to conduct courses in history and civics and the state's board of education, quoting extensively from the *Gobitis* opinion, instituted a mandatory flag salute exercise. All teachers and pupils were required to salute the flag every morning: "refusal to salute the Flag [will] be regarded as an Act of insubordination, and shall be dealt with accordingly." The penalty for insubordination was expulsion; readmission was denied until the child or teacher complied with the act. Any expelled child was considered "unlawfully absent"; the state could thus proceed against the student as a delinquent, and the student's parents were liable for prosecution (the penalty was fifty dollars and/or thirty days in prison). Since the statute applied to all schools in the state, public and private, expelled children who refused to salute were thoroughly excluded from attending school until they recanted and submitted to the flag salute.

The Barnette family, members of the Jehovah's Witnesses religious sect, attempted to persuade the board of education to delete the compulsory aspect of the salute—as the *Gobitis* opinion suggested—but while the salute requirement was amended somewhat it still came into conflict with Exodus, and its admonition to the Witnesses not to bow down to graven images. (Some modifications were made based on complaints from the Boy Scouts and the PTA that the salute was similar to the Nazi gesture; the Witnesses, however, rejected a substitute pledge which said, "I have pledged my unqualified allegiance to Jehovah, the Almighty God, and to his kingdom, for which Jesus commands all Christians to pray. I respect the flag of the United States and acknowledge it as a symbol of freedom and justice to all. I pledge allegiance to it.") They brought suit in the federal district court in West Virginia, asking the court to issue a restraining order prohibiting the state from enforcing the flag salute statute. The court, taking judicial notice of the events since the *Gobitis* decision was announced, did not follow *Gobitis* as precedent and issued the injunction. The state board of education brought the case to the Supreme Court on appeal.

The issues argued before the Supreme Court in 1943 were those that had been discussed in *Gobitis* three years earlier. The board of education lawyers urged the Court to dismiss the injunction because the law and board of education regulations were actions taken under the state's police power and did not violate fundamental civil or religious rights. The lawyers for Barnette, headed by Hayden C. Covington (who argued most of the eighty seven cases brought to the Supreme Court by the Jehovah's Witnesses), asked the Supreme Court to overturn *Gobitis* and reaffirm the fundamental importance of the Bill of Rights in a constitutional system of free government.

THE OPINIONS

THE MAJORITY: MR. JUSTICE JACKSON

"This case calls upon us to reconsider a precedent decision, as the Court throughout its history often has been required to do," wrote Jackson at the beginning of the opinion. Before proceeding to a discussion of *Gobitis*, he reviewed the child salute controversy with a view toward distinguishing that conflict between liberty and authority from others that had come before the Supreme Court.[50]

By way of getting to the essential question for the Supreme Court in *Barnette*—whether a state power exists in the Constitution to compel such a flag salute ceremony—the Jackson opinion presented six broad statements (dicta) to buttress its subsequent discussion of *Gobitis*.

First, the majority recognized that the freedom the Jehovah's Witnesses asserted did not bring them into collision with rights of others, a conventional situation that called historically for state resolution. The refusal to salute was different; there was no interference with or denial of rights of others to do so. The refusal was, additionally, a peaceful and orderly one.

Second, the statute was in effect censorship or suppression of certain types of belief, and "it is now commonplace that censorship or suppression of expression of opinion is tolerated by the Constitution only when the expression presents a clear and present danger of action of a kind the state is empowered to prevent and punish." In this controversy, compulsion is invoked without any allegation that remaining passive during the ritual creates a clear and present danger. "To sustain the compulsory flag salute we are required to say that a Bill of Rights which guards the individual's right to speak his own mind, left it open to public authorities to compel him to utter what is not in his mind."[51]

A third general observation of the majority was that throughout history, from the early Christians to the Quakers, small religious sects have been persecuted for their refusal to respect symbols of authority in symbolic ceremonies. "Objection to this symbolic form of communication when coerced is an old one, well known to the framers of the Bill of Rights."[52]

The majority opinion pointed out that scholarly information had indicated that, as an educational device, the flag salute does not instill patriotism in students who have no religious or other reasons for refusing to salute the flag in school. In an article in the *Journal of Educational Research*, Professor Olander, quoted by the Court majority, examined the educational impact of the salute and found "a rather pathetic picture of our attempts to teach children not only the words but the meaning of our flag salute."[53] If the attempts did not work with students who had no religious misgivings about the salute, what could the consequences be on the Jehovah's Witnesses?

A fifth point was to distinguish the issues raised in this case from those raised in the 1934 Court decision in *Hamilton* v. *Regents*. *Hamilton* involved college students attending a state university in California who protested compulsory military training courses. They argued that their religious convictions prohibited them from taking these required courses. The Supreme Court disagreed, stating that the requirement was a legitimate exercise of the state's police powers: creation of a cadre of reserve officers in case of national emergency or war. Jackson argued, however, that college attendance was optional and that if the students objected to the requirements, they could attend another college. The West Virginia situation was inapposite: school attendance was compulsory, and all schools in the state were required to salute the flag daily. Jehovah's Witness children did not have the options these college students had; therefore *Hamilton* was not a controlling precedent in the flag salute controversy.

After making these general points, the majority went to the essence of the legal and constitutional problem. This issue, Jackson wrote, "does not turn on one's possession of particular religious views or the sincerity with which they are held—*the issue is whether the state has the power to make the salute a legal duty.*"[54] *Gobitis* assumed the existence of such a power; in determining whether *Gobitis* was wrong, the Court had to examine, rather than take for granted, whether the state of West Virginia (or the town of Minersville, Pennsylvania) had the power to coerce Jehovah's

Witnesses to salute the flag. The essential question was "whether such a ceremony, touching matters of opinion and political attitude, may be imposed upon the individual by official authority under powers committed to any political organization under our Constitution."[55] In arriving at the answer, the Jackson opinion discussed the four basic assumptions of the *Gobitis* opinion, refuting each in turn.

First, *Gobitis* put the controversy in stark Lincolnesque terms, when it asked whether a government must be too strong for the liberties of a people or too weak to maintain its own existence. Put in those terms, the *Gobitis* majority opted in favor of strength. However, pointed out the majority in *Barnette*, the government is a government of limited powers.

Government of limited power need not be anemic government . . . . Without promise of a limiting Bill of Rights it is doubtful if our Constitution could have mustered enough strength to enable its ratification. To enforce these rights today is not to choose between weak government over strong government.[56]

Observance of the limitations of the Constitution will not weaken government in those fields appropriate for its exercise of power.

As for the argument in the 1940 opinion that interference by the Supreme Court in educational matters was not appropriate because it would make the Court the school board of the nation, the Jackson opinion pointed out that the Fourteenth Amendment, incorporating the First Amendment, applies to the states and its agencies. A board of education and school board are such agents of the state, and "they must operate within the confines of the Bill of Rights. . . . There are village tyrants, but none who acts under color of law is beyond the reach of the Constitution."[57]

A third basic point Frankfurter made in *Gobitis* was that the Supreme Court justices lacked controlling competence in the field of education and that the public political arenas were the places where the problems should be resolved. Jackson's opinion differed dramatically: "The very purpose of a Bill of Rights was to withdraw certain subjects from the vicissitudes of political controversy, to place them beyond the reach of majorities and officials and to establish them as legal principles to be applied by the courts. One's right to life, liberty, and property, to free speech, a free press, freedom of worship and assembly, and other fundamental rights *may not be submitted to a vote; they depend on the outcome of no elections.*"[58]

The First Amendment rights can be restricted only to "prevent grave and immediate danger to the state which the state may lawfully combat." The duty of the Court is not to defer automatically to legislative action but to apply the Bill of Rights to such questions: "This duty . . . does not depend upon our marked competence in the field where the invasion of rights occurs." The task of the Court is to transplant eighteenth-century rights into a turbulent twentieth century:

We act in these matters not by authority of our competence but by force of our commissions. We cannot, because of modest estimates of our competence in such specialties as public education, withhold the judgment that history authenticates as the function of this Court when liberty is infringed.[59]

Finally, Jackson pointed out that the heart of the *Gobitis* opinion was the notion that, in the name of national unity (which was the basis of national security and the very existence of the state), the state can take any action it feels appropriate to achieve that end. "Upon the verity of this assumption depends our answer in this case," stated the majority opinion in 1943.[60]

The majority opinion disagreed with that assumption of unlimited power in the name of national security and unity. Dissidents and eccentrics are a part of civilization, and they are not too great a price to pay for continued liberty. "Those who begin the coercive elimination of dissent (Romans, Germans, Russians, Turks, etc.) soon find themselves exterminating dissenters," said Jackson. "The First Amendment was designed to avoid these ends —coercion—by avoiding these beginnings." Government by consent of the governed denies those in power the legal opportunity (given the presence of the Bill of Rights) to coerce the public.

If there is any fixed star in our constitutional constellation, it is that no officials, high or petty, can prescribe what shall be orthodox in politics, nationalism, religion or other matters of opinion or force citizens to confess by word or act their faith therein. If there are any circumstances which permit an exception, they do not now occur to us.[61]

The action of the school board was unconstitutional, the Court concluded: "Compelling the flag salute and pledge transcends constitutional limitations on their power and invades the sphere of intellect and spirit which it is the purpose of the First Amendment to our constitution to reserve from all official control."[62] *Gobitis* was thus overruled, and the judgment of the lower Court enjoining the enforcement of the West Virginia statute was affirmed.

Concurring Opinion: Mr. Justices Black and Douglas

Justices Black and Douglas concurred separately in order to "make a brief statement of reasons for our change of view" since their vote in *Gobitis*.[63] Their basic reason for voting to validate the flag salute in the 1940 case was their "reluctance to make the Federal Constitution a rigid bar against state regulation of conduct thought inimical to the public welfare. Long reflection convinced us that although the principle is sound, its application in the particular case was wrong."[64] The freedom of religion of the Jehovah's Witnesses was infringed upon by the compulsory flag salute. While religious faiths do not free individuals from the responsibility of obeying laws, laws that infringe upon religious opinion must be "imperatively necessary to protect the society as a whole from grave and pressingly imminent dangers or which, without any general prohibition, merely regulate time, place or manner of religious activity."[65]

The two justices backed off from the restrictive judicial self-restraint view of Frankfurter they had followed in 1940.

Decision as to the constitutionality of particular laws which strike at the substance of religious tenets and practices *must* be made by this Court. The duty is a solemn one and in meeting it we cannot say [that failure of the Jehovah's Witnesses to salute and pledge allegiance] creates a grave danger to the nation. Such a statutory exaction is a form of test oath, and the test oath has always been abhorrent in the United States.[66]

For Black and Douglas, the statute was a handy implement for disguised religious persecution; as such, it was inconsistent with the Constitution.

Concurring Opinion: Mr. Justice Murphy

Justice Frank Murphy, the third of the recanters in *Opelika*, stated that although he understood the motivation of the Court in *Gobitis*—himself included—"there is before us the freedom of belief, the freedom to worship according to one's conscience," which is more important than judicial restraint, symbolism, and so forth. "Reflection has convinced me that as a judge I have no loftier or responsibility than to uphold that spiritual freedom to its furthest reaches."[67]

Murphy was "impelled to conclude that the flag salute is not necessary to the maintenance of effective government and orderly society."[68] Its benefits do not outweigh the costs involved: the invasion of freedom and individual privacy. The real unity of America, he concluded, lies in freedom of conscience and opinion and in persuasion.[69]

Dissenting Opinion: Mr. Justice Frankfurter

Justices Roberts and Reed "adhered to the views expressed by the Court in Gobitis and are of the opinion that the judgment below should be reversed."[70]

In a long, stinging twenty-five-page dissent, Justice Frankfurter's opinion developed four interdependent arguments: self-restraint of the justices, historical aspects of religious liberty in America, the flag salute law, and the consequences of the judgment of the majority in *Barnette*. It was a powerful statement of judicial self-restraint. Its opening lines have become classic:

One who belongs to the most vilified and persecuted minority in history [Frankfurter was a Jew] is not likely to be insensible to the freedoms granted by our Constitution. Were my *purely personal attitude relevant* I should wholeheartedly associate myself with the general libertarian views of the Court's opinion, representing as they do the thought and action of a lifetime. But as judges we are neither Jew nor Gentile, neither Catholic nor agnostic. . . . As a member of the Court I am not justified in writing my private notions of policy into the Constitution, no matter how deeply I cherish them or how mischievous I deem their disregard. . . . It can never be emphasized too much that one's own opinion about the wisdom or evil of a law should be excluded altogether when one is doing one's duty on the bench.[71]

Wisdom and constitutionality are two separate issues, believed

Frankfurter. The judge can be concerned only about the latter, however unwise he personally thought the policy. Wisdom was best left to the legislators. The Court can look only into the reasonableness of the legislation, not its wisdom or folly. If the legislation is foolish, then legislators, "the guardians of liberty," must change the statute: the full play of the democratic process takes place without judicial involvement argued Frankfurter.[72] If judges involve themselves in these controversies, they are no different from the lawmakers, and then they should "be made directly responsible to the electorate."[73]

Judges should be very diffident in setting their judgment against that of a state in determining what is and what is not a major concern, what means are appropriate to proper ends, and what is the total social cost in striking the balance of imponderables.[74]

When employing judicial review, judges must show extreme deference to those who have the responsibility for making the laws. Quoting Chief Justice John Marshall, Frankfurter said: "There is a two-fold rule for the Court: 'never seek to enlarge the judicial power beyond its proper bounds, nor fear to carry it to the fullest extent that duty required.' "[75]

A second theme, interwoven into all the rest, was Frankfurter's view of religious liberty. The First Amendment emphasized toleration but "minorities may disrupt society."[76] The Constitution, Frankfurter went on to say, did not create new privileges for religious sects; it merely gave religious equality. There is no freedom from conformity to civil law simply because of the religious beliefs and dogmas one held. The essence of the religious freedom guarantee was that no religion shall either receive the state's support or incur its hostility. In short, religion was outside the sphere of government.[77]

This led to his third point: the flag salute statute was, repeating his contention in *Gobitis,* an action that promoted good citizenship. National allegiance is within the domain of governmental authority. While it may be folly (and Frankfurter admits further on that indeed it was folly), it was not an unconstitutional folly. And, even though it be folly, an individual cannot restrict community action simply because of religious convictions.

Frankfurter insisted again that "the flag salute suppressed no belief nor curbs it."[78] *Hamilton* was precisely like the flag salute situation; "I find it impossible to differentiate between the two cases."[79] Both states were legislating for the development of future citizens, he argued. Furthermore, until the present case, in the four previous occasions where the Court took note of the flag salute issue (three were per curiam notes, the fourth was *Gobitis*), all but one, fourteen judges including Hughes, Brandeis, and Cardozo, agreed with Frankfurter on the legitimacy of the statutes.

Frankfurter bitterly complained that because of the addition of two new judges and the deciding shift of opinion of other justices, the old policy was destroyed.

What reason is there to believe that they or their successors may not have another view a few years hence? Is that which was deemed to be of so fundamental a nature as to be written into the Constitution to endure for all times to be the sport of shifting winds of doctrine? Of course, judicial opinions, even as to questions of constitutionality, are not immutable. As has been true in the past, the Court will from time to time reverse its position. But I believe that never before these Jehovah's Witnesses cases has this Court overruled decisions so as to restrict the powers of democratic government.[80]

Finally, and unusual in a Court opinion that generally limits itself to the facts of the case, Frankfurter tried to estimate the consequences of the *Barnette* decision. With over 250 various religious sects in America, Frankfurter saw *Barnette* opening up the floodgates of litigation dealing with issues such as science versus religion in the schools, prayers in the school, textbook loan programs, and sectarian texts. This litigation would disrupt the social life of communities and place the courts in the middle of political controversies.[81]

This led to his final plea for judicial self-restraint. With this type of litigation, courts come very close to sensitive areas of public affairs: "As appeal from legislation to adjudication becomes more frequent, and its consequences more far reaching, judicial self-restraint becomes more and not less important, lest we unwarrantly enter social and political domains wholly outside our concern."[82]

He concluded by admitting the folly of the flag salute. "Of course patriotism cannot be enforced by the flag salute. But neither can the liberal spirit be enforced by judicial invalidation of illiberal legislation."[83] Democracy calls for citizens to sear the conscience of legislators to achieve social and political justice. The consequence of such judicial self restraint was that if the religious minority failed to achieve the change, consistent with the Constitution, then, absent judicial intervention, the "illiberal legislation" remained in oppressive effect.

THE OVERTURN DECISION: CRAFTSMANSHIP OR FIAT?

The *Barnette* opinion was favorably received by the legal community, the public, and the press. *Barnette* "removed a blot upon the nation."[84] The Jackson opinion overturned *Gobitis*, and beyond that action, it emphatically affirmed a basic principle of the Bill of Rights: certain rights and liberties are not subject to the tantrums of popular majorities on national, state, or local levels that attempt to deny these fundamental rights to small sects within the larger community.

Before evaluating the *Barnette* overturn itself, which has to be judged a craftsmanlike, statesmanlike product of fallible judges, a discussion of the basic differences between the Frankfurterian theory of majoritarian absolutism and the Jackson/Stone consitutionalist position is required.[84] This cleavage between the two diametrically opposed views went far beyond the flag salute controversy. Their differences went directly to the essence of the judicial role in American society.

Frankfurter, throughout his life as scholar and justice of the Court, held that in a democracy judges have only the power of moral persuasion. Consequently the scope of their power is narrow. They must constantly defer to legislative and executive —political—actions, no matter how foolish and unwise these policies are. Unless political actions, challenged properly in court, are patently offensive or shock the conscience of the judge, they must stand, for judges cannot substitute their views of the proper remedy for a social malady for those of legislators.[85] The Supreme Court is not the guardian of the people's rights and liberties.

If judges want to become involved in political adjudication, if they want to defend the poor and oppressed and those otherwise miserably treated by society, they should become politicians. Judges are not result oriented, they are goal oriented; and the goal of the judiciary is to resolve only cases and controversies that could be resolved by judges without injuring the reputation of the judiciary.

Judges must put aside their personal predelictions and prejudices and mechanically rule on cases, always mindful of the fact that in a democracy the political actors are the guardians of liberty. In the political arenas, not in the courtroom, panaceas to social, political, religious, economic, and cultural ills can be offered, debated, legislated, and discarded or modified. In a political democracy, oligarchic federal judges are marginal political actors at best. Democracy's failure would be signaled when the judiciary became greatly involved in the pressing social and political issues of the day. Democracy fails when courts must continuously overturn allegedly illiberal actions of legislators. Therefore Courts must constantly defer to all legislative actions, regardless of whether these acts deal with economic regulation or religious regulation and coercion.

If life is an experiment and democratic government the noblest experiment in social living, then one must accept fallibilism and occasional unrectified illiberal actions of political actors. One hopes that wisdom will come to the political actors; but it must not come to the political actors from the judges. Supreme Court justices are not Kadi sitting on mountain tops hurling thunderbolts in the form of judicial opinions down to the masses. Unlike Platonic wise men, all justices must refrain from interfering with the actions of the community struggling in the cave with the shadows of reality.

Evil and folly exist now, existed in the past, and will continue to exist in the future. That is the tragedy of the human condition. Judges must "never seek to enlarge judicial power beyond its bounds," said Frankfurter, quoting Chief Justice John Marshall, "nor fear to carry it to the fullest extent duty required." For Frankfurter, the bounds of judicial power were narrow. Unlike Marshall, who was unafraid to use the judicial power to its fullest, Frankfurter was philosophically disinclined to do so. Better to allow a sect such as the Jehovah's Witnesses to be compelled to act or to be punished for not acting in light of their religious beliefs than have the Court dispense fiat from the bench in an attempt to resolve the controversy. Better that liberty be stilled for a small segment of the society—a troublesome sect of religious fanatics—than have democracy destroyed totally by having the judges instead of the political actors make policy.

The Jackson/Stone opinions presented a radically different perception of the judicial function. All men, including the Supreme Court justices, are fallible. Legislators have acted "illiberally" and cruelly in the past toward minorities and have deprived them of fundamental human rights. The Bill of Rights was an attempt to prevent these cruelties from continuing in the new republic. It contained certain basic personal protections—speech, press, association, petition rights, and religious freedom—that could not be denied to segments of the population by majority votes of others in the community. If they occurred and litigation arose in the courts, it was the duty of the judges to listen to the arguments and, the competency of the judges aside and irrelevant, decide the constitutional issue on the merits. Their commissions and the oath of office they took as judges—to do justice to rich and poor alike—required no less of them. Judges must listen and examine and decide; if they cannot do that task, then they ought to leave the bench.

Although judges ought to show deference to economic and social practices of the government (see the *Darby* opinion), they must also carefully scrutinize legislative actions that touch upon and infringe personal rights guaranteed individuals in the society by virtue of the Bill of Rights. No actor of the governments, national and state, school board member, or the president of the United States, is beyond the reach of the Constitution with its enumerated limits on political power. And, as Marshall said in *Marbury* in 1803, "It is the duty of the Judiciary to say what the law [of the Constitution] is."

The Supreme Court is the highest judicial body in the society, thus the justices are final—and fallible. The Frankfurter view suggested that liberties could only be maintained and protected in the political arena. The Jackson/Stone position was that the political processes throughout history have been sources of oppression and that the judges must give life and meaning to the Bill of Rights by hearing cases and attempting to ensure the prominence of these rights. Judges are duty bound to see that these rights are not tampered with by popular majorities unless the tampering is legitimate, accomplished through amendments to the Constitution itself.

Chief Justice John Marshall knew this when he wrote that the judges "must never forget that it is a Constitution we are expounding for the ages." Judges have the power as well as the duty to examine questions such as those brought to the Supreme Court by the Jehovah's Witnesses. Not to have heard the case on the merits would have been a rejection of the responsibilities of the justices in the constitutional system.

Employing the judicial power in the flag salute cases meant examining carefully rather than assuming that a state could coerce citizens to salute the flag. Frankfurter's opinion for the majority in *Gobitis* did not carefully examine whether Pennsylvania and Minersville officials could in fact and under law coerce people to violate their religious principles or face fine, jail, and exclusion from school. The *Barnette* overturn was reasonable because of its more realistic views on the importance and prominence of the First Amendment guarantees (Frankfurter, dissenting, argued that there was no difference between economic and political rights in the Constitution and that all protections were on an equal level and could not be ranked in terms of importance) and because of its view that judges are responsible for examining the substance of arguments involving allegations that these rights were infringed.

"Law's essentially contradictory nature accurately mirrors the tragic condition of human existence," wrote Jan Deutsch.[86] What the two views of the judicial function have described is the fundamental nature of the existential dilemma, and reality, of judging in a democracy. If, as Frankfurter suggests, judges must defer to popular assemblies and the popular will, then there is a good possibility that personal liberties will fall victim to passing prejudices. That is the human condition, he reflected. But judges must not become involved in political and social thickets regardless of the evil that exists and regardless of the personal convictions of the judge. Judges must be onlookers, passive observers of this existential reality. Hoping for wisdom, they cannot suggest remedies for the society; the remedy will not be accepted and will damage the societal "training in liberty" irreparably. If liberty is destroyed today, the hope is that it will return, strengthened, in the future.

"The Federal system works only if judges in reaching decisions attempt in good faith to reconcile the conflicting values of the community."[87] If, as Jackson and Stone suggested (agreeing with the observation), the function of courts is to examine cases and controversies carefully that come before the Court and attempt to resolve them, then the consequences for the Court would be constant litigational bombardment by groups who have been allegedly denied justice. Justices of the Supreme Court would become participants in the social and political dilemmas of the country; they would be an integral part of the democratic political process. They would attempt to balance the liberties guaranteed in the Bill of Rights with the countervailing demands for societal orderliness by constructing such doctrines as "clear and present danger" or "preferred status." Because of the position the Court has in society, the justices, though fallible had to hear these cases.

Since Marshall's time, the Jackson/Stone dilemma has been the reality for the Supreme Court. Throughout most of American history, the Court has expounded on the meaning of the Constitution and on the meaning of its principles. The *Gobitis* majority did not examine; it assumed the validity of the state action. As such, it did not function as the Court traditionally has in our history. *Barnette* rectified that erroneous perception of the judicial function. The fact is that until leaders of people become philosophers or philosophic wise men become politicians, there will be folly, suffering, and violations of the Bill of Rights. Given this essence of the human tragedy, the Jackson/Stone position is the realistic view of the judicial function. Often the courts will be powerless, ill advised, persuaded by fear and anger, but they can be the difference between the maintenance of civil and personal liberties and the loss of these constitutional guarantees.

RIGHTNESS OF THE OPINION

Three justices in *Opelika* admitted error two years after *Gobitis* was announced. Reflection had persuaded them that the Court must examine the constitutional dilemma raised by the Jehovah's Witnesses because certain rights cannot be subjected to the demands and pressures of the political marketplace. *Gobitis* was wrongly decided and had to be overturned. Government is one of limited powers, the overturn suggested, and that perception was correct. The Bill of Rights was erected to be a barrier against wrongs committed by government.[88] There was no unlimited right and power of government to coerce without overriding grave reasons for violating human rights. Courts had to examine the reasons for the state's interference with these personal liberties to determine whether there was a clear and present danger to the community that warranted a restriction of First Amendment rights.

The earlier opinion had met with thorough disapproval from the legal community because it neglected to examine the substantive question of whether the state had the power to coerce. With the justices's recantation in *Opelika*, the precedential value of *Gobitis* plummeted. To deal with this admitted error by a third of the Court, the Court had to consider overturn. *Gobitis* could not be ignored, nor could it be distinguished. In order to decide the fate of *Gobitis* the Court in *Barnette* raised the questions the Frankfurter opinion did not ask in 1940. It did so in a statesmanlike manner, thoroughly discussing the constitutional issue and carefully examining important constitutional clauses. Error was present, the majority stated in *Barnette:* error in perceptions of reality and error in perceptions of the historic role of the Court in American politics and law. *Barnette* restored rightness to the common law and in so doing has to be considered a reasonable judgment.

DEFINITENESS OF THE OPINION

Changed conditions in society and throughout the world were factors in the overturn of *Gobitis*. The 1940 opinion was written during a period when fear of foreigners and fear of impending attack by Germany motivated public behavior. Reflection and perception of the impact of the *Gobitis* decision on religious freedoms and the impact with respect to unlimited powers given to the state led to the overturn. By 1943 many Americans, including the justices of the Court, were aware of the logical consequences of allowing the state to compel people to act in a certain manner. New facts came to light highlighting the indefiniteness of the *Gobitis* opinion with respect to remedies for state oppressiveness. In addition, with the recantation in *Opelika,* the impact of *Gobitis* became clouded, and its status as precedent became indefinite and uncertain. Though the uncertainty was created by judicial admission of error, the uncertainty had to be cleared up. It was cleared up by judicial overturn.

Gobitis was unclear and indefinite because the majority had refused to answer the essential questions raised by the Witnesses. Clarity is a characteristics of a reasonable opinion of the Court. By not answering the substantive questions raised by the attorneys, the opinion suffered in quality. By assuming but not discussing the legitimacy of the state's power to compel certain behavior, the Frankfurter opinion left open and unanswered basic constitutional questions that were answered in *Barnette.*

PRINCIPLES

The Frankfurter opinions, for the majority in *Gobitis* and dissenting in *Barnette,* showed some disdain for the rights of the Jehovah's Witnesses, exclaiming that such sects were troublemakers and dangerous to the community's social order. However, the concept of religious toleration in America developed in response to such attitudes by officials toward Quakers, Protestants, Jews, and others. At the time of the writing of the Bill of Rights, religious toleration was a controversial matter, and the framers of the First Amendment believed that the protections of the First in the area of religion put an end, theoretically, to the debates. Americans could not be compelled to accept a state religion, for there was to be a separation between church and state. If they were not to be compelled by a state religion, they could not be compelled or coerced by the state to do something against their religious beliefs unless the national security were in grave jeopardy.

Justice Jackson's statement that "if there is any fixed star in our constitutional constellation, it is that no official, high or petty, can prescribe what shall be orthodox in politics, nationalism, or religion, or other matters of opinion," was a reflection of the vision and intent of the framers of the Constitution. The ideal element's concern for religious toleration was ignored by the Court in *Gobitis*. *Barnette* returned to constitutional principles and, in so doing, overturned the first, preliminary, judgment of the Court in the flag salute controversy.

SUMMARY

The child labor case was overturned because a later Court (essentially the same one that overturned *Gobitis*) believed that it was the consequence of judicial interference with the legitimate actions of the legislative assemblies. In economic matters, judges ought to defer the popular majorities. The principles of the Constitution lent credence to that argument of the Court in *Darby*.

In the flag salute cases, the 1940 opinion of the Court reflected the view that judges must defer to legislative assemblies when the object legislated was religious in character. *Gobitis* emphasized a theory of judicial restraint that removed the Court from controversies involving personal freedoms. *Barnette* perceived that there are crises when judicial deference is legitimate (economic experimentation), but there are also controversies where the Court must intervene on behalf of the basic personal guarantees of the Constitution. There is no conflict between the judgment of the Court in *Darby* with the *Barnette* decision. Historically judges have involved themselves in these controversial issues of human freedoms. *Gobitis* went against tradition and principle. *Barnette* returned the Court to the maelstrom of democratic politics, where it has always been. It was a reasonable overturn.

NOTES

1. *Cantwell* v. *Connecticut*, 310 U.S. 296 (1940).

2. Francis Heller, "A Turning Point for Religious Liberty," *Virginia Law Review* 29 (September 1943): 440.

3. A. T. Mason, *Harlan Fiske Stone: Pillar of the Law* (New York: Viking Press, 1956). p. 599.

4. Henry J. Abraham, *The Judiciary: The Supreme Court in the Governmental Process,* 4th ed. (Boston: Allyn and Bacon, 1977), p. 92.

5. "Religious Freedom and Compulsory Saluting of the Flag," *University of Cincinnati Law Review* 14 (1940): 445.

6. Edward F. Waite, "The Debt of Constitutional Law to Jehovah's Witnesses," *Minnesota Law Review* 28 (March 1944): 217; see also Alfred Wilke, "Jehovah's Witnesses Define Religious Freedom," *University of Detroit Law Review* 7 (1943): 15.

7. Madaline Remmlein, "Constitutional Implications of Compulsory Flag Salute Statutes," *George Washington Law Review* 12 (1943): 71–74.

8. Ibid.

9. Mansur Tinsley, "Legal Considerations Behind Statute's Requiring a Salute to the Flag," *Rocky Mountain Law Review* 12 (Spring 1940): 202–203.

10. Ibid.

11. Remmlein, op. cit., p. 73.

12. *Gobitis* v. *Minersville School Board,* 21 F. Supp. 581 (1938).

13. See *Leoles* v. *Landers,* 302 U.S. 656; *Hering* v. *Board of Education,* 303, U.S. 624; *Gabrielli* v. *Knickerbocker,* 306 U.S. 621; *Johnson* v. *Deerfield,* 306 U.S. 621.

14. *Minersville School District* v. *Gobitis,* 310 U.S. 586 (1939), at 588.

15. Ibid., at 590.

16. Ibid., at 593.

17. Ibid., at 594–95.

18. Ibid., at 597–98.

19. Ibid., at 598.

20. Ibid., at 599.

21. Ibid., at 600.

22. Ibid., at 602.

23. Ibid., at 605.

24. Ibid., at 606.

25. Heller, "Turning Point," p. 447.

26. Ibid., p. 448.

27. These cases, decided in the 1920s and 1930s, dealt with the right of parents to send children to private schools and foreign languages in those private schools (*Myers* and *Society of Sisters*), canvassing on the streets, (*Schneider* and *Cantwell*), freedom of speech for radical political groups (*Herndon* and *De Jonge*), and rights of labor to use public facilities (*Hague*).

28. See "Compulsory Flag Salute," *New York University Law Review* 18 (1940): 126–127; "The Flag Salute Case," *Washington Law Review* 15

(1940): 266; Louis Levene, "The Compulsory Flag Salute," *Cornell Law Quarterly* 26 (1940): 127.

29. Charles Carpenter, "Religious Freedom," *Southern California Law Review* 14 (1940): 58.

30. Tinsley, op. cit., p. 207.

31. Alta Toomey, "Compulsory Flag Salutes and Religious Liberty," *University of Detroit Law Review* 4 (Fall 1940): 38–39.

32. *Colegrove* v. *Green*, 328 U.S. 549 (1946).

33. See Tinsley, op. cit., p. 207; "Compulsory Flag Salute."

34. Wilke, op. cit., p. 16.

35. Tinsley, op. cit.; Heller, op. cit.; William Anderson, "Freedom of Religion and Conscience," *Michigan Law Review* 39 (1940): 151–152.

36. "Religious Freedom," p. 447.

37. *California Law Journal, Cornell Law Quarterly, Georgia Law Journal, International Juridical Association Bulletin, Michigan Law Review, Missouri Law Review, New York University Law Review, Columbia Law Review, St. Johns Law Review, Southern California Law Review, Cincinnati Law Review, Detroit Law Review, Washington Law Review, Harvard Law Review, Yale Law Journal.* The three journals that supported the flag salute statutes were *George Washington Law Review* in 1938 and the *Michigan Law Review* and *St. Johns Law Review* in 1939.

38. Heller, op. cit., p. 450.

39. Ibid., p. 459.

40. *Times, Newsweek,* and *New Republic;* see Heller, op. cit., p. 455.

41. Ibid., p. 457.

42. Ibid.

43. Ibid., p. 449.

44. *Jones* v. *Opelika*, 316 U.S. 584 (1941).

45. Ibid., at 598.

46. Ibid., at 615.

47. Ibid., at 619.

48. Ibid., at 623–624.

49. Quoted in Heller, op. cit., p. 459.

50. *West Virginia Board of Education* v. *Barnette*, 319 U.S. 624 (1943), at 630.

51. Ibid., at 634.

52. Ibid., at 633.

53. Ibid., at 631, n. 12.

54. Ibid., at 634.

55. Ibid.

56. Ibid., at 636–637.

57. Ibid., at 638.
58. Ibid.
59. Ibid., at 640.
60. Ibid.
61. Ibid., at 641.
62. Ibid.
63. Ibid., at 643.
64. Ibid.
65. Ibid., at 644.
66. Ibid.
67. Ibid., at 645.
68. Ibid., at 646.
69. Ibid.
70. Ibid., at 642–643.
71. Ibid., at 646–647.
72. Ibid., at 649.
73. Ibid., at 651.
74. Ibid., at 652.
75. Ibid., at 668.
76. Ibid., at 653.
77. Ibid., at 654.
78. Ibid., at 664.
79. Ibid., at 665.
80. Ibid., at 659–661.
81. Ibid., at 666.
82. Ibid., at 670.
83. Remmlein, op. cit., p. 77
84. Heller, op. cit., p. 451.
85. See Ball, *Vision and Dream*, passim.
86. Jan G. Deutsch, "The Jurisprudence of Affirmative Action: A Post Realist Analysis," *Georgetown Law Journal* 65 (April 1977): 881.
87. Ibid., p. 888.
88. See Ball, *Vision and Dream*, chap. 4.

5 The Free Speech in Shopping Center Cases

Since the Revolutionary period, American society has emphasized the importance of a well-informed public. Democratic theory posits this as a basis for societal advancement, and Supreme Court decisions since 1940 have consistently recognized the right of access to public streets and parks for the purpose of exercising the First Amendment rights.[1] The rights in the amendment are meaningless unless the speaker (or picketer or religious proselytizer) can communicate his or her message to the public. For some, the method of communication is the mass media; the wealthy protester can advertise on radio, television, and in the press to reach the public. For the less affluent in American society, the method used to reach the public is confrontation—peaceful for the most part—on the streets, in parks, and at other public places so that the message can be transmitted via signs, handbills, singing, kneelings, and so forth to the passing public.

The Supreme Court in *Hague* v. *CIO* (1939) said that

wherever the title of streets and parks may rest, they have immemorially been held in trust for the use of the public and, time out of mind, have been used for purposes of assembly, communicating thoughts between citizens, and discussing public questions. Such use of the streets and public places has from ancient times been a part of the privileges, immunities, rights, and liberties of citizens.[2]

Thus it has been the case that citizens may use the public forums to express themselves on matters of public concern—within certain limits established by the Supreme Court.[3] The subject of this chapter involves the question of whether citizens have a right to use private forums, in particular, the large private shopping centers that have proliferated throughout suburban America since 1945, in their attempts to communicate to the public within these commercial places of business.

Since the 1930s the Supreme Court has dealt extensively with questions relating to the nature of expression (is the wearing of an armband protected expression? is the burning of a draft card protected symbolic speech? is picketing a form of free expression?) and with questions that invited discussions as to the nature of governmental interference with such types of expression.[4] With the shopping center cases, the Supreme Court had to examine the outcome of a clash between "two cherished constitutional principles," free speech (protected by the First and Fourteenth amendments) and private property (protected by the Fifth and the Fourteenth amendments).[5] Neither constitutional principle is absolute: free speech can be curtailed if there is an imminent danger to the society; private property, throughout the history of the Anglo-Saxon, American law, has always been encumbered by the existence of zoning ordinances, nuisance laws, rent control, and similar measures.[6]

When the two rights conflict, neither of them absolutes in themselves, the Court has to weigh the importance of each and, consistent with the essence of the fundamental law, come up with a reasonable judgment in the light of factors discussed in chapter 2. The essential question raised in the various cases decided by the Supreme Court from *Marsh* v. *Alabama* (1946) to *Hudgens* v. *National Labor Relations Board* (1976) was whether an owner of private property open for business and extending an invitation to the public to enter the property could prohibit some of these people from exercising their First Amendment rights of free expression on his or her property. Was the shopping center, open to the public and providing various services, an alternative forum—a private one—that paralleled the public forum with respect to providing citizens with a means to reach other citizens?

In all these cases protestors—religious, economic (labor unions), and political—expressed their views through distributing handbills or through picketing on the private property (the shopping center) open to the public. In all cases they were asked to leave and/or were enjoined by state courts from protesting because of the character of the forum and the unwillingness of the owner to give these speakers the forum for expression of their ideas. Litigation arose because the protesters believed they had a right—constitutional and, in economic protests, statutory—to speak out on these private premises.

In every one of these cases that came to the Supreme Court, the majority and dissenters engaged in heated philosophical debate regarding the sanctity or lack of sanctity of private property, the concept of state action, and the right of freedom of speech and expression. The decisions attempted to deal with the essential question of free speech on quasi-public property by attempting to balance these two constitutional rights. The right of protest was not the issue in these cases: the place of protest was the question.

The protesters' cases rested on the fact that the freedom to speak in the public forum extended to private establishments that served a public purpose. These establishments, shopping centers, were not private property exclusively; neither were they public property. They were somewhere in between the two extremes: quasi-public or quasi-private. In any event, since they did affect the public, they could be used as forums for the expression of ideas. This argument was based on the 1946 decision of the Supreme Court in *Marsh* v. *Alabama*. Succeeding relevant cases were *Logan Valley Plaza* (1968), which creatively extended the rationale of *Marsh* to include shopping centers into the state action concept; *Central Hardware* and *Lloyd* which condemned *Logan Valley* to death; and *Hudgens* v. *NLRB* (1976), which executed *Logan Valley*. The important question is whether *Hudgens* was a reasonable, statesmanlike piece of judicial craftsmanship.

FREEDOM OF EXPRESSION ON PRIVATE PROPERTY TO *LOGAN VALLEY PLAZA,* 1968

"Gracie Marsh was the cornerstone for *Logan Valley Plaza* and progeny," said one legal scholar correctly.[7] Marsh was a Jehovah's Witness involved in litigation in Alabama. The case came to the Supreme Court during its 1945 term and involved the company-owned town of Chickasaw, Alabama. The managers of the town, employees of the Gulf Shipbuilding Corporation, had refused to allow Marsh to preach her religious views on the streets of the privately owned town. She did so nevertheless and was arrested by a deputy sheriff—paid by the company to serve as the town's policeman—for violating the Alabama trespass statute (entering and remaining on the premise of another after having been told not so to remain). The conviction of trespass upheld in the state courts, Marsh appealed to the Supreme Court (*Marsh* v. *Alabama*).

The question for the Court was whether a state can impose criminal sanctions on persons who distribute religious literature on the streets of a company-owned-town, contrary to the wishes of management, and not fall afoul of the limits of the First Amendment. In an opinion written by Justice Hugo Black, the Court said that such action was not consistent with the commands of the Constitution. He argued that, given the primacy of the First Amendment freedoms, a public municipality cannot pass such an ordinance completely banning the distribution of literature from its streets fronting the business district. And, he asked, if a public municipality cannot pass such an ordinance completely banning free expression, can a private town act any differently? The answer: if the private town has "all the characteristics of any other American town" and "if it did not function differently from any other town," except that legal title belonged to the private company, then that private town was "the equivalent of the public municipality and was subject to the same constitutional restraints."[8] If Chickasaw has residential buildings, sewers, sewerage disposal plants, business shops, a post office, deputy sheriffs, and a regular shopping center where persons may use company-owned sidewalks and streets to enter shops, then it is the "functional equivalent" of the public town. As such it cannot bar, ban, or prosecute speakers who wish to use the streets for expression of ideas.

In so concluding that the private town was in effect public, Black expanded the concept of state action. Indeed one commentator called *Marsh* an "aberration from conventional constitutional theory."[9] The idea of state action developed as a consequence of the passage of the civil rights amendments and the passage of civil rights legislation by the national Congress in the 1860s and 1870s. Invalidating many of these statutes, the Supreme Court in 1883 maintained that the Fourteenth Amendment prohibited certain actions of sovereign states and the agents of these states; the amendments did not extend to purely private action.[10]

Black's position in *Marsh* was an extension of the state action concept. His view was that when actions of private persons rise to the level of state functions—that is, when private acts assume the nature and characteristics of governmental acts—these private acts were, in reality, state functions. The town's functions and characteristics constituted state action, and therefore the company town could not evade the requirements of the First Amendment. Black found state action necessary to preserve First Amendment freedoms from destruction by economic and social changes (company towns) unforeseen by the writers of the Bill of Rights.[11]

In a democracy the public has a right to be informed; that right is a fundamental one in a representative system of government. Property owners, except under certain circumstances, cannot ban free expression on their property. Ownership does not mean absolute domination. In obiter dicta—statements made by the Court off the basic point of law—Black said that "the more an owner, for his advantage, opens up his property for use by the general public, the more do his rights become circumscribed by the statutory and constitutional rights of those who use the property."[12] The task of the Court, in such conflicts, is to balance the property rights against freedom of expression, mindful of the fact that the First Amendment has a preferred position in the hierarchy of constitutional values. Freedom of speech and religion "enjoy a 'preferred position' in our society," and property rights do not "justify a state's permitting a corporation to govern a community of citizens so as to restrict their fundamental liberties and the enforcement of such a restraint by the application of a state statute."[13]

Given the fact that the physical characteristics and functions of the private town were no different from those of a public municipality, the rationale in *Marsh* was that such private property assumed the characteristics and therefore the responsibilities of any public town. Private property was, in reality, public property and subject to the constraints of the First Amendment as discussed in *Hague* v. *CIO.* The most important question left unanswered by Black, to be answered in *Logan Valley Plaza* and its progeny, was the extent to which the property owner had to open his or her property to the general public before an individual could exercise constitutional rights free from fear of arrest for trespass. When did private property loses its privacy and become a quasi-public place of business where protesters could meet and express themselves?[14]

Justice Black's reasoning was not acceptable to Justice Frankfurter. Not willing to accept the dictum and its portent of possible problems to come before future courts, Frankfurter concurred. He argued that a company town was a town: "title to property controls the property relations; it cannot control issues of civil liberties which arise precisely because a company town is a town as well as a congeries of property relations."[15]

The dissenters, like Frankfurter, were concerned about Black's views on private property and hoped that the decision would be limited as precedent to its unique set of facts. They (Associate Justice Reed wrote the opinion, joined by Justice Harold Burton and Chief Justice Vinson) dissented because they felt that Marsh could have taken her religious message to a "nearby public highway and under our decisions she could rightfully have continued her activities thirty feet parallel from the spot she insisted upon using."[16] With the majority reaffirming the principle of preferred First Amendment rights, the dissenters pointed out that one "may remain" on private property against the will of an owner and contrary to the law of the state so long as the only objection to his presence is that he is exercising an asserted right to spread there his religious views."[17]

That was not the case; the dissenters misrepresented the majority position on the basic question of law. But it was, as Justice Holmes suggested in 1927, "the usual last resort of [dissenting] constitutional arguments."[18] The Black position held that only when the private property took on all the characteristics of a public municipality serving the needs of the general public would the facility lose its privacy status.

The action of the managers of the Alabama town was "state action/function" and subject to the restraints of the First and Fourteenth amendments. They were performing the "full spectrum of municipal services and *stood in the shoes of the state.*" The precedential point of law was that the private facility had to perform all the functions of the public municipality for First and Fourteenth amendments to be relevant and applicable to that special type of state function phenomenon.

The irony of the *Marsh* situation was that the company town was rapidly disappearing in America at the very moment the Court in 1945 was deciding the case. (It is suggested that the replacement for the company town has been the migrant farm compound, a genuinely dirty, dilapidated facility that provides food, clothing, shelter, provisions, protection for the migrant workers. An important question that has been raised since the 1960s is whether *Marsh* and its progeny have relevance with respect to the rights of organizers to speak with the workers in these compounds—which are private property.)[19] And, at the time of the *Marsh* decision, the phenomenon of the suburban shopping center was in the process of dramatically taking hold in America. The next time *Marsh* would be employed as point of law would be with respect to the status of the shopping center vis-à-vis the rights of people to express themselves in or in front of one.

The controversy between expression and property rights came to the attention of the Supreme Court in the 1956 case of *National Labor Relations Board* v. *Babcock and Wilcox Company.* Congress's intent in passing the 1935 National Labor Relations Act was to regulate under a uniform federal law all labor disputes affecting the free flow of commerce. The National Labor Relations Board had primary jurisdiction in handling conflicts between management and labor, preempting state and local courts as well as federal court jurisdiction.[20] Section 7 of the act allowed workers to bargain collectively and to meet and organize for that purpose; section 8 prohibited management from preventing union members from meeting with employees in an attempt to organize them. Any unfair labor-management practice would be examined and adjudicated before the NLRB, with appeal from the board's decision to the Federal Court of Appeals and then to the Supreme Court.

Babcock and Wilcox management had refused to allow nonemployee union organizers permission to distribute union literature on the company-owned parking lots. The union had filed charges under section 8 of the NLRA with the board, accusing the company of violating the section 7 right of employees to organize without employer hindrance. The board concluded that there was an unfair labor practice and, consistent with section 8, issued a cease and desist order. The company took the case to the circuit court and won its argument when that court ruled that there was no unfair action by the management. The board then took the case to the Supreme Court where the Court, in an opinion written by Justice Reed (who was a dissenter in *Marsh*), upheld the judgment against the NLRB.

On statutory grounds the Court unanimously held against the board because there were other alternatives available to union organizers for communicating with the employees about the benefits of unionization. The plant was close to the towns where the workers lived, and literature could have been distributed there. In addition, newspapers and radio stations were available sources that could have been used to contact the employees. The board had overlooked these channels of communication and had therefore overextended itself in that ruling. The board had claimed that the only public place near the factory was a dangerous right of way in heavy traffic congestion. The parking lots and the walkway from them to the gatehouse were the only "safe and practicable" places for the distribution of the Union's literature.[21]

In response, Justice Reed stated that an employer may post his property against non employee distribution of union literature if reasonable efforts by the Union through other available channels of communication will enable it to reach the employees with its message and the employers notice or order does not discriminate against the Union by other distribution.[22]

An accommodation between organizational rights and property rights "must be obtained" by the NLRB with as little destruction of one as is consistent with the maintenance of the other. The balance struck by the Court was an important one: the property owner did not have to offer private property to union organizers if there were alternative sources through which it could reach its audience.

Marsh and *Babcock and Wilcox* had set up three separate criteria for balancing private property interests with the exercise of free speech:

1. Traditional notion: the First Amendment does not attach to privately owned property.
2. The *Marsh* standard: the First Amendment applies to private property that is the functional equivalent to public property.
3. The *Babcock and Wilcox* standard: section 7 of the NLRA may, if there are no other sources of communication available, require an owner to relinquish certain ownership interests in favor of the union's right to effective communications with employees.

In *Logan Valley Plaza* and its progeny, the Court joined *Marsh* and *Babcock and Wilcox*. In so doing, the 1968 Court confused these three separate criteria (*Marsh* was not mentioned at all in *Babcock and Wilcox*) in the *Amalgamated Food Employees Union Local 590* v. *Logan Valley Plaza*, turning what was essentially an NLRB statutory construction case into a constitutional decision by the Warren Court majority. The Court turned a labor case into a constitutional question of the first magnitude.[23]

THE *LOGAN VALLEY PLAZA DECISION*, (1968)

By the 1960s the suburban shopping center, accounting for almost 50 percent of consumer sales in America, had taken firm hold. Shoppers, entering the shopping center "as freely as they traverse a downtown shopping district," flocked to these mammoth commercial centers.[24] So, too, did labor picketers, religious believers, and political dissidents. As the shopping center displaced the city business district and as the community's economic and social business district activities passed from public to private property, the constitutional debate regarding free expression in this shopping center phenomenon increased.[25] *Marsh* and other cases had, in effect, created a constitutional easement for freedom of expression on public property and private property that rose to the level of state function (or, in labor situations, where the private property was the only means of reaching the workers). *Logan Valley Plaza*, the first shopping center case to come before the

Supreme Court, was a watershed case because the justices confronted the fact that the traditional idea of the small town-large city business center had to be revised because of the growing economy and the mobility of Americans after World War II.

The case, which came to the Supreme Court from Pennsylvania, confronted the justices with this question: can peaceful union picketing of a business enterprise located within a private shopping center be enjoined by a state court on the ground that the action constituted an unconstitutional invasion of the property rights of the owners of the land upon which the shopping center was located?

Weis Supermarket, located in the Logan Valley Plaza shopping center, employed nonunion employees. The owner prohibited union organizers from trespassing or soliciting his workers on the covered porch fronting the store—five feet wide and forty feet long—and in the parking area adjacent to his establishment. The market was about 400 feet from one public road and 350 feet from another public thoroughfare. These two roads were the only public entrances to the private establishment. The union picketers were employees of a competitor of Weis.

After ten days of picketing on the private property, Weis and the Plaza managers instituted an action at equity in the court of common pleas in Pennsylvania. An injunction was issued prohibiting picketing on the property. The effect of the injunction was that the union workers had to distribute their information to the workers from the public streets some distance away from the market or picket from berms, high beside the public roads. Arguing that the effect of the injunction was to deny the union freedom of expression, the petitioners failed in their appeal to the supreme court of Pennsylvania; they appealed to the United States Supreme Court.

Logan Valley Plaza was primarily a labor case (and indirectly it was also a civil rights confrontation). Under the NLRA, unions have the right to organize nonunion workers and can bring the issue to the attention of the NLRB if there is an alleged unfair practice against labor by management. Justice Thurgood Marshall, for a six-man majority, with Justice Douglas concurring, did not deal with the case's labor and picketing rights of labor under the NLRA. He did not raise the question of whether the NLRA preempted the field in this area of labor-management relations. (One of the dissenters, Justice John Harlan, raised these points.)

Instead he invalidated the state injunction by appealing to the *Marsh* rationale (but not the facts). Arguing that the modern shopping center, similar to the downtown business district, could not immunize itself from picketers and protesters by creating a *cordon sanitaire* of parking lots around the buildings, Marshall creatively applied the *Marsh* dicta to the *Logan Valley Plaza* fact situation. Peaceful picketing in a private facility generally open to the public and inviting the public into its malls and stores, provided there are no alternative areas of communication available, is protected by the First and Fourteenth amendments. "The shopping center here is clearly the 'functional equivalent' of the business district in *Marsh*," wrote Marshall—without noting that the company town in Alabama was the functional equivalent of the public town because Chickasaw provided all the services that a public municipality would ordinarily provide its citizens.[26]

The majority opinion maintained that there was no difference between the company town business district and "property functioning as a business district" even though the shopping center did not provide all the facilities of a public municipality. Recognizing that "First Amendment freedoms could be seriously jeopardized by a lack of an effective forum for free expression in the suburbs," Marshall reasoned that the mall and shopping center serve as the business block for suburbanites in America.[27] People freely assemble in the mall, private but open to all, and the owners cannot, through local trespass laws, exclude members of the public from exercising their First Amendment rights. If the mall was not ordinarily open to the public, maintained Marshall, it would not rise to the level of a "state function." But when property opens to the general public, its private character disappears, and the First Amendment becomes a viable restraint on the activities of the management of the property.[28]

"Perhaps in deference to the strong dissents," the Marshall opinion limited the holding of *Logan Valley Plaza* to its facts.[29] The justice reserved the question of "whether picketing which was not directly related in its purpose to the use to which the shopping center was being put" would be protected by the First Amendment.[30] The majority opinion, therefore, created the "related to the use test" with regard to free expression in a private shopping center: free speech could be exercised for a purpose generally consonant with the use to which property was actually put.[31]

One major problem, for the dissenters and concurring justices, with the majority opinion was the analogy Marshall drew between the company town and the private shopping center. Marshall suggested that the center was the "functional equivalent" of the business district of the company town, For Justices Douglas, Black, White, and Harlan, this was the critical point in the case and with respect to the precedential value of the *Logan Valley Plaza* decision.

Justice William O. Douglas, Jr. concurred: "While Logan is not dedicated to the public use *to the degree* of the corporate town in *Marsh*, it is clear that respondents have opened the shopping center to public uses."[32] The picketing related directly to the shopping center's business activities and policies and, although some of the aspects of the injunction were invalid, Douglas believed that the union organizers should have been restrained from interfering with the workers while they were working and from interfering with delivery men and customers. There should have been some restraints, but picketers and protesters cannot be totally banished from the private property.

Private property cannot become a sanctuary immune to protests if that property is opened to the public. The Pennsylvania courts should be given the opportunity, believed Douglas, to "fashion a decree that will ensure non-interference with customers and employees while enabling union members to assemble sufficiently close to Weis's market to make effective the exercise of their First Amendment rights."[33] Douglas was suggesting a balancing view, the view suggested by the Court in *Marsh* and especially in *Babcock and Wilcox*. The shopping center was not quite the same as the business district of the company town, but it had lost enough of its private character to warrant peaceful picketing within certain boundaries.

Justice Hugo Black dissented. As the jurist who wrote the majority opinion in *Marsh*, Black was concerned by the way in which the majority erroneously misused the precedent. The two situations were not analogous, he argued; there was little resemblance between *Marsh* and *Logan Valley Plaza*. The former was a company town that replicated all the functions of the public municipality, thus assuming the level of "state function/action," and was therefore subject to constitutional prohibitions. Logan Valley Plaza was a private shopping center that performed few of the functions of a company or public town.

Black agreed that picketers had a constitutional right to speak and distribute literature, but he also believed that they did not have a constitutional right to compel Weis to furnish them a forum to do so on his property. The Constitution, Black urged, recognized and supported the concept of private ownership of property. The Marshall opinion had, in effect, taken that private property and given it to the protesters. If the Court acts in this manner, then, bitterly suggested Justice Black, the Court ought to award Weis just compensation for the property taken by such fiat.[34]

On procedural grounds, Justice Harlan dissented. He believed that the case was a labor-management problem covered by the NLRA and the board established under that legislation. He urged that the NLRB issue be raised and he believed that it was a conflict subject to resolution through application of relevant statutes and was not the constitutional question the majority opinion had created.[35] He was of the opinion that the case should have been vacated and remanded to the courts for disposition along those lines. Section 7 of the NLRA was the answer to the shopping center case, and the precedent of *Babcock and Wilcox* was relevant; the Supreme Court wrongfully used the First Amendment and "state function/action" concept in *Logan Valley Plaza*.

Justice Byron White, the third dissenter in *Logan Valley Plaza*, also argued that the shopping center was not the equivalent of the business district of a company town but was a collection of stores, driveways, and lanes leading from one public street to another. These paths led to a parking area for the convenience of customers. This was not the fact situation in *Marsh*, concluded White. Furthermore, he argued, the rationale of the Marshall opinion for the majority, if followed to its logical conclusion, would allow all forms of nonobstructive picketing and protesting, religious and political, under the First Amendment. These protests on private property would take place under *Logan Valley Plaza's* rationale "although the activities may have no connection whatsoever with the views of the plaza's occupants or with the conduct of their business."[36] White was expressing a fundamental fear of the consequences of the 1968 decision of the Warren Court. (This fear of uncontrolled and expanded use of *Logan* was a basic factor in the decision of the Court, a few short years later, to curtail *Logan Valley* dramatically.)

In 1968 a creative majority used the *Marsh* precedent, itself a creative exercise in judicial adjudication, to protect freedom of expression. It maintained that the shopping center, given the nature of American growth and economic expansion, was the new downtown business district. Picketing could take place because there was no other way the protesters could reach their potential audience. The legal creativity of the Court was challenged—mildly by the concurrence of Justice Douglas and sharply by the three dissenters.

EVALUATION AND IMPACT OF *LOGAN VALLEY PLAZA*

EVALUATION

The *Logan Valley Plaza* decision did not meet with universal acclaim. Some argued that although the Court reached out to handle the conflict on constitutional grounds, it should have been dealt with, as suggested by dissenting Justice Harlan, as a labor case: "The NLRB should act in this area; if a shopping center is affected with the public interest and [rises to the level of state action], when is a business not a public business?"[37] Still others condemned the Marshall decision for misreading *Marsh*: the shopping center did not have all the attributes of the business district in the company town; therefore it was not performing a state function and was still private property.[38] "Whether the Union has won a pyrrhic victory is a question not yet resolved," wrote another critic of the majority opinion.[39]

What the Marshall opinion in *Logan Valley Plaza* attempted to do, however incrementally the balancing came off, was to cope with the reality of the shopping center in America. The questions and criticisms come down to whether this reality was the functional equivalent or a replacement of the downtown business district. If the suburban center was the equivalent or the replacement of the public downtown area, which were open to picketers and protesters parading on the public streets directly in front of the private establishment, did the constitutional free expression easement apply to the private center? The Marshall majority cautiously answered in the affirmative, limiting the opinion to the facts of the case.

Justice Marshall took judicial notice of the postwar growth of these centers and their phenomenal success, the result of the population's movement away from the central cities.[40] At the beginning of this development, the center was a strip of small shops, usually anchored by a supermarket. Then the community center (the strip, a supermarket, and a junior department store or discount store) developed. The first type of center generally was between 30,000 to 100,000 square feet and could accommodate between 5,000 to 40,000 people. The community center was a center with between 100,000 and 300,000 square feet and could accommodate between 40,000 and 150,000 shoppers.

In the mid-1950s, regional centers developed, complexes usually anchored by one or more major department stores and containing anywhere from thirty to sixty smaller stores providing all types of goods and services. In the 1960s these regional centers were enclosed in climate-controlled, air-conditioned comfort. They ranged anywhere from 300,000 square feet to over a million square feet and could handle from 150,000 to almost one-half million shoppers. These regional malls have become the new downtowns. In the twenty one largest cities in America, the malls lying adjacent to them account for over 50 percent of the retail trade business. In the Boston area, 70 percent of the retail trade is handled by these private malls; in St. Louis, over 67 percent of the trade is conducted in the plazas.[41] They have been referred to as the "piazzas of America"; in them, one can live, sleep, be entertained, eat, work, shop, receive medical and dental treatment, exercise, mail letters, join the army, navy, or air force, and, in a Cleveland suburban center, be buried. For the eighty million suburbanites in America, the shopping center has become a way of life, and most of their social, banking, and economic activity is centered around the private mall. If the mall provided housing—and some of the latest malls do—it would be a complete city (all of them have security police and fire protection).[42]

The *Logan Valley* majority acknowledged the reality of the shopping center as the district of suburbia where business and pleasure was transacted and where the freedom of expression had to extend if the First Amendment was not to be a victim of modern economic and demographic changes in America. The linchpin of the opinion, therefore, was the fact that, for precedential purposes, the shopping center was the functional equivalent of the business district of the private town-public town and was not immune to the commands of the First Amendment.[43] Just as Black, in *Marsh*, had balanced the property rights of the company against the right of the Jehovah's Witness to express herself freely on religious matters and communicate these views effectively to a public, the majority in *Logan Valley*, carefully and creatively, balanced the rights of labor picketers against the rights of the owner of the plaza and concluded that there was a right to free expression for a purpose generally consonant with the use to which the property was actually put.

The essence of the judicial function is to examine the controversy before the Court and, consistent with the basic principles of the Constitution, to arrive at a reasoned judgment that resolves the controversy. In this activity the Court has to take into consideration changing social and economic conditions. This the Warren Court majority did; the reality of the shopping center was noted and the decision, limited to the facts, was reached. However, *Logan* was criticized by the dissenters, legal commentators, and the business community in general, and its impact on case law was spotty.

THE IMPACT

Logan Valley Plaza, given the majority's concern for the continued vitality of freedom of speech in modern America and its concern that that fundamental right would be seriously jeopardized by the lack of an effective forum for speech in the suburbs, "declared a constitutional easement to picket on private property commensurate with the degree to which an owner effectively transferred his property into a public forum."[44] Although some state courts (in Kansas and Ohio) did not apply *Logan Valley* positively, others vigorously extended the rationale. California and Washington courts allowed antipollution picketers to communicate with customers in private malls. New York courts allowed picketing to take place in private bus terminals, and Minnesota courts allowed campaign workers to distribute literature in a shopping plaza. In all of these cases, management had refused to allow these activities to take place; in all, the Warren Court denied certiorari (thus letting stand the state courts' expansion of *Logan Valley Plaza*).[45]

In less than two years, however, the majority that decided *Logan Valley Plaza* had evaporated. Chief Justice Earl Warren resigned in 1968, Abe Fortas in 1969. The six-man majority was reduced to a minority of four—assuming that the two men President Richard Nixon appointed took positions antithetical to the Marshall position. Warren E. Burger and Harry Blackmun, the two new Court justices, joined in 1971 by Justices Lewis Powell (who replaced Justice Hugo Black) and William Rehnquist (who replaced Justice John M. Harlan), formed the basis of what came to be called the Nixon Court. With the changed composition of the Court, it was not long before *Logan Valley Plaza* was reappraised. This reappraisal came during the 1971 term when the Court heard arguments in *Central Hardware* v. *NLRB* and *Lloyd Corporation* v. *Tanner*. (It subsequently announced both decisions on the same day.)

The first of the two free expression versus private property rights cases involved labor pickets who were attempting to contact employees of a hardware store in the parking lot adjacent to the store itself. *Central Hardware* v. *NLRB*, like *Babcock and Wilcox* in 1956, involved the interpretation of sections 7 & 8 by the NLRB. The union, claiming rights under section 7, used a private parking lot next to Central Hardware to solicit petitioner's employees in order to get them to join the union.

When the owner ordered the picketers and organizers off the parking lot—his property—the labor organizers filed an unfair labor practice charge against management before the NLRB. Union charged management with a practice in violation of section 8 of the act. The board found in favor of the union and issued a cease and desist order, which, was upheld by the Fifth Circuit Court of Appeals. Central Hardware then appealed that judgment to the Supreme Court and, in an opinion written by Justice Lewis Powell, the Supreme Court vacated and remanded in the light of the 1956 *Babcock* precedent.

There was certainly a conflict between private property rights and free expression presented in the litigation, Powell admitted. Under section 7 of the NLRA, property rights must yield to organizational rights of labor but that management acquiescence must be "only temporary and minimal. The continual use of the parking lot by Union organizers turned to a violation of property rights because it was ongoing and not merely organizational and necessary to facilitate the exercise of employee Section 7 rights."[46]

Logan Valley Plaza was not relevant in this case, stated Powell. The 1968 opinion involved a large commercial shopping center, which had displaced certain functions of the traditional business block. However,

before an owner of private property can be subjected to the commands of the First and Fourteenth Amendments the privately owned property *must assume to some significant degree* the functional attributes of public property devoted to public use. First and Fourteenth Amendments are limitations on state action, not on action by the owner of private property used only for private purposes.[47]

The parking lot did not assume the functional attributes of private property devoted to public use. To so hold, argued Powell, would "constitute an unwarranted infringement of long settled rights of private property protected by the Fifth and Fourteenth Amendments."[48]

Justices Marshall, Brennan, Stewart, and Douglas dissented. (These four were the residue of the six-man *Logan* majority.) Their view was that the NLRB should have used the Court's judgment in *Babcock* to guide it in *Central Hardware*. There should have been remand without discussing and deciding the constitutional issues.[49] Their concern about the Court majority's examination of the constitutional question was deeply sincere, for in the companion case of *Lloyd Corporation* v *Tanner*, the majority had raised the constitutional issues raised by the Marshall majority in 1968 and by Black in 1945 and had drastically narrowed the precedential impact of both, especially *Logan Valley Plaza*.

Lloyd posed the question that the Marshall opinion had not directly answered and that Justice White in dissent had raised: did protesters have a First Amendment right to use the shopping center as a forum for expressing ideas having nothing to do with the general purposes of that private forum? (Justice White, who dissented in *Logan Valley Plaza*, was the swing vote in these two decisions.)

Lloyd came to the Court from Portland, Oregon, and involved picketing by an anti-Vietnam war group, the Call to Resistance. They were protesting the war in an enclosed, air-conditioned mall built on property given to the developers by the city in the 1950s and in which twelve security guards, deputies of the Portland, Oregon, police force patrolled, armed with weapons. Reversing the direction of case law in the states and sharply curtailing the impact of *Logan Valley*, the five-man majority attacked the rationale of the 1968 decision with respect to the question of free expression on private property.

Marsh and *Logan* had reflected a view that private property assuming a state function lost the traditional immunity the Constitution afforded nongovernmental private action and was subject to the commands of the First and Fourteenth amendments. In *Lloyd* Justice Powell's opinion redirected the case law on that subject.

The Call to Resistance was distributing handbills in the interior mall of the Lloyd Center, owned by the Lloyd Corporation. The corporation had a no-handbill regulation but it had allowed the American Legion to sell poppies and allowed the Salvation Army, the Boy Scouts, Volunteers for America, and presidential candidates to distribute information while denying this privilege to the antiwar group, gubernatorial candidates, and a Jewish service group. Prohibited from expressing themselves in the mall on the war, the group sought in federal district court a decree enjoining the corporation from blocking their actions.

The antiwar group won on the merits in the lower federal court by using the arguments developed by the Court majorities in *Marsh* and *Logan Valley Plaza*. Judge Harold Solomon wrote the opinion for the lower court:

I find the mall the functional equivalent of a public business district. Marsh and Lloyd are identical except that Marsh was a company town and Lloyd a shopping center. I do not believe the distinction should cause a different result.[50]

The corporation appealed to the Supreme Court, essentially arguing in the words of counsel for the American Retail Federation (who filed an amicus curiae brief):

Owners may deny the use of their premises to those who wish to use the premises for First Amendment activities unrelated to the purpose for which the public is invited except where no reasonably effective alternative means of communication is available.[51]

The Supreme Court, in an opinion written by Justice Powell, reversed the finding of the lower federal court and concluded that the Lloyd corporation had a right to ban handbill distribution from its mall. The shopping center, noted Powell, was interlaced by public streets and roads; it was not cut off from public municipal facilities and roads. Furthermore being open to the public is not the functional equivalent of a business district. The majority in *Logan Valley* "incorrectly interpreted" *Marsh* with respect to the question of whether a private shopping center was the functional equivalent of the business district in the Chickasaw, Alabama, town. Powell stated that the 1968 Court erred when it said that "whenever a privately owned business district serves the general public its sidewalks and streets become the functional equivalent of similar public facilities."[52]

The views of the late Justice Black were reaffirmed by Powell, but there was no direct overturn of *Logan Valley*. The Constitution, Powell argued, "by no means requires such an attenuated doctrine of dedication of private property to public use [that *Logan Valley* suggested]."[53] In *Marsh* the owner of the company town was "performing the full spectrum of municipal powers and stood in the shoes of the state." This was not so in *Logan Valley Plaza* or in *Lloyd:*

> Private property does not lose its private character merely because the public is generally invited to use it for designated purposes. Few would argue that a free standing store, with abutting parking spaces for customers, assumes significant public attributes merely because the public is invited to shop. Nor is size alone the controlling factor. The essentially private character of the store and its privately owned abutting property does not change by virtue of being large or clustered with other stores in a modern shopping center.[54]

Justice Powell rejected the "functional equivalency" standard discussed in *Logan Valley Plaza,* called the linchpin of that decision, because the Marshall opinion had shown an insufficient regard for the rights of private property. "This Court has never held," noted Powell, "that a trespasser or an uninvited guest may exercise general rights of free speech on property privately owned and used non discriminatorily for private purposes only."[55] However, Powell did not overturn *Logan Valley Plaza.* He did employ the standard discussed by Marshall in 1968: the "related to the use" test. (The Marshall opinion, limiting itself to the facts, stated that free speech could be exercised for a purpose generally consonant with the use to which the property is out.)

Speech on the premises of a private shopping center was permitted, said Justice Powell, if it was related to the use of the mall and if there were no adequate alternatives available. Powell thus put together part of the *Logan* majority opinion and a significant portion of the statutory judgment, *Babcock and Wilcox,* to resolve the conflict. The group protesting the war in Vietnam was not like the union organizers attempting to reach the Weis workers; there were adequate alternative avenues of communication available to the war protesters in the *Lloyd* case that were not available to the union picketers in *Logan Valley Plaza.* Thus *Logan Valley* was distinguishable from *Lloyd Corporation.*

The dissenters—Marshall, Douglas, Brennan, and Stewart—angrily responded to the majority opinion. Justice Marshall, the author of *Logan Valley,* wrote the dissenting opinion. He was highly critical of the fact that the majority opinion ignored what, to Marshall, was the basic theme running through *Marsh* and *Logan Valley:* the right of property owners to limit free expression on their property diminishes as the property assumes functions of the state and becomes the business district of the community. (It is important to note that Justice Powell used this precise argument in *Central Hardware* when he argued that the parking lot did not assume "to some significant degree the functional attributes of public property devoted to public use.")

If anything, *Lloyd Center* was more analogous to the conditions in *Marsh* than was *Logan Valley Plaza,* argued Marshall. Lloyd was larger, had more professional services, and had a police force with full municipal powers.[56] He also argued that the mall was the only place where the political protesters "had reasonable access to all of Lloyd Center's patrons." Marshall could see no logical reason for the Court's distinguishing between speech related to center activities and speech unrelated to center stores."[57] (Neither could the Supreme Court for, a few months later, in *Police Department* v. *Mosely,* it invalidated a municipal ordinance that allowed labor picketing but no other type of protest on grounds that such an action violated the equal protection clause of the Fourteenth Amendment.) Many persons do not have access to news media, and for them picketing is the only means of conveying their ideas to the public:

The only hope that these people have to be able to communicate effectively is to be permitted to speak in those areas in which most of their fellow citizens can be found. One such area is the business district of a city or town or its functional equivalent. And this is why respondents have a tremendous need to express themselves within Lloyd Center.[58]

The *Lloyd* opinion carefully distinguished the fact situation in Oregon from the situation in Pennsylvania in the 1960s. While rejecting the functional equivalency standard in *Lloyd* (though employing it in *Central Hardware*), it did retain the other "relatedness of speech" standard as well as employing a standard from the statutory, NLRB case of *Wilcox* (1956). *Logan Valley Plaza* was, in effect, "moribund,"[59] "critically undermined,"[60] "drained of vitality,"[61] and "left stranded on a philosophical limb."[62]

Lloyd was not only bewildering and inconsistent; it was called, analogous to the labels given to the child labor case of 1918, "an anachronism in its own time."[63] In an attempt to save *Logan Valley,* Powell was thoroughly inconsistent. He used the rationale of *Logan Valley Plaza* to remand the *Central Hardware* case, yet in *Lloyd* he discarded the "functional equivalency" standard as inconsistent with the principles of the Constitution.

In the attempt to halt the extension of the *Logan* doctrine for fear of consequences to the rights of private property, Powell rejected the reality of the shopping center in American life. His language, comparing the million-square foot regional center servicing a potential 450,000 patrons to a small grocery store, "indicates an unwillingness on the Court's part to deal with some new and basic changes in American economic life caused by the modern mall shopping center."[64] The Powell opinion failed to take into consideration the fact that the shopping center has replaced the business district; it totally ignored the social, public function of the center in the name and on behalf of protecting property rights.

The most important and most "unsettling"[65] feature of these 1971 decisions of the five-man majority was their failure to recognize the reality of the shopping center accompanied by their realization of the "modern context in which First Amendment rights are to be exercised."[66] Justice Marshall's view in *Lloyd* with respect to the majority was perhaps on the center target: "it was *Logan Valley* itself that the Court finds bothersome."[67] Ominously and prophetically, Marshall concluded by stating that "Logan Valley is binding unless and until it is overruled."[68] If *Lloyd* condemned the 1968 opinion to death, the execution took place during the 1975 term of the Supreme Court.

THE OVERTURN OF *LOGAN VALLEY PLAZA: HUDGENS* v. *NLRB* (1976)

FACTS AND CONSTITUTIONAL ISSUES

Hudgens involved a labor dispute that developed in Atlanta, Georgia. The North DeKalb shopping center contained over sixty retail stores leased to various businesses. All were located off an enclosed mall and could be entered only through that interior mall in the center. Butler Shoe Company warehouse employees had struck management and had picketed the company's retail outlets in the Atlanta area. Union employees picketed the Butler store in the center until halted by a threat of trespass arrests from Hudgens, the manager of the private center.

The NLRB found the Hudgens threat to be a violation of sections 7 and 8 and issued a cease and desist order. Hudgens appealed the judgment in the Fifth Circuit Court of Appeals at about the time *Lloyd* was decided by the Supreme Court. The fifth circuit remanded the case to the NLRB with instructions to the board to act in light of the Supreme Court decisions in both *Lloyd* and *Central Hardware*. The board in turn handed the issue to an administrative law judge who made findings of fact and, based on *Babcock* and *Logan Valley*, found that Hudgens had committed an unfair labor practice in violation of section 8.

Since *Babcock* involved different factual circumstances—unionization activities with respect to nonunion employees—the fifth circuit combined the *Babcock, Logan Valley*, and *Lloyd* rationales to come to its conclusion that Hudgens did violate section 7 when he prohibited the labor picketing in the center. "The fifth circuit's mingling of legal standards was foreseeable by the Supreme Court's initial failure in *Logan Valley* and *Lloyd* to separate labor issues from First Amendment questions."[69]

Hudgens appealed the circuit court judgment to the Supreme Court. He and the union both used *Babcock and Wilcox* as precedent; the union argued that there were no alternative avenues of communication available to the striking workers, and Hudgens held that there were other available forums of communication through which the union could make its case to the public. The third party in the suit, the NLRB, was concerned about parity for section 7 rights within the NLRA and argued before the Court that these statutory rights were in reality First Amendment guarantees. The board's argument was that the First Amendment's free speech standard should govern and that section 7 was an example of congressional activity directed toward the protection of labor's rights of free expression.[70]

THE PLURALITY OPINION:
MR. JUSTICE STEWART

Justice. Stewart, joined by Justices Blackmun and Rehnquist, wrote the judgment of the Court. Justice Powell, joined by Chief Justice Burger, wrote a concurring opinion. Justice White wrote another concurring opinion. Justices Marshall and Brennan, dissenting, wrote a fourth opinion in the case. In *Hudgens* the Court was so split that the eight men participating in the case (Justice Douglas had recently retired, and his replacement, Justice John Paul Stevens, did not participate in the arguments and in the writing of the decision) wrote four opinions; the Court could not muster a majority behind any one of these four rationales developed.

Justice Stewart's opinion took note of the confusion the lower courts had with conflicting legal standards and attempted to clear the debris: "The history of this litigation has been a history of shifting opinions on the part of the litigants the Board, the Court of Appeals. It has been a history . . . of considerable confusion, engendered at least in part by decisions of this Court that intervened during the course of the litigation."[71] For Justice Stewart the fundamental question raised was whether the conflict was to be resolved "under the criteria of the NLRA alone, under a First Amendment standard, or under some combination of the two."[72] In answering that question, he made "it clear now, if it was not clear before, that the rationale of *Logan Valley* did not survive the Court's decision in the *Lloyd* case."[73] (Justice Stewart voted with Marshall in *Logan Valley Plaza* and dissented with Marshall in *Lloyd*. Unlike the three justices who switched in the flag salute cases, Justice Stewart did not mention his conversion at all in *Hudgens*. None of the other opinions made mention of the Stewart change of position. Stewart did not say whether new wisdom compelled the move; it was a silent unexplained conversion, a mute admission of error.)

While *Lloyd* did not directly overrule *Logan Valley*, and a large segment of the former opinion was devoted to distinguishing the differences of fact between the two cases, "the fact is that the reasoning of the Court's opinion in Lloyd cannot be squared with the reasoning of the Court's opinion in Logan Valley Plaza."[74] The ulti-

mate holding and rationale in the 1971 case "amounted to a total rejection of the holding in Logan Valley Plaza."[75] The rationale of the
Marshall majority opinion in 1968 did not survive *Lloyd.*

> If a large self contained shopping center is the functional equivalent of a
> municipality, as Logan Valley held, then the First and Fourteenth Amend-
> ments would not permit control of speech in such a center to *depend on the
> speech's content.* Conversely, it follows that if respondents in Lloyd did not
> have a First Amendment right to enter the shopping center to distribute
> handbills concerning Vietnam because it was a private place, then re-
> spondents in the present case did not have a First Amendment right to enter
> this shopping center for the purpose of advertising their strike against the
> Butler Shoe Company. We conclude, in short, that under the present state
> of the law, the constitutional guarantee of free expression has no part to
> play in a case such as this.[76]

In reaching this conclusion, Stewart employed the concept of
state action/function discussed by Black dissenting in *Logan Valley*
and by Powell in *Lloyd.* "The present state of the law was that private property becomes public when it takes on *all* the attributes of a
town." If the shopping center does not take on all these attributes,
then it remains private property, and the "constitutional guarantee
of free expression has no part to play in a case such as this."[77] First
Amendment rights, concluded Stewart, are restraints on state and
federal governments, not on the owner of private property. For
Stewart, who viewed these questions quite differently in 1968 and
in 1971, the "right of a private property owner to control the use of
his premises predominates over free expression in Hudgens."[78] Put
simply, the shopping center was not dedicated to public use in the
same way that a municipality's business district was used.

Concluding the opinion, Stewart returned to the fundamental
question and answered it by stating that the "rights and responsibilities in this case are dependent upon the NLRA which calls for
the Board to seek a proper accommodation between union and private property rights with as little destruction of one as is consistent
with the maintenance of the other."[79] The judgment of the Fifth Circuit Court of Appeals was vacated and the case remanded so that
the NLRB could consider the conflict under the statutory requirements of the NLRA. *Logan Valley Plaza* was no longer a case on

point and could not be employed by the board, or by the courts, in any future rulings.

CONCURRING OPINION: MR. JUSTICE POWELL (WITH CHIEF JUSTICE BURGER)

Justice Powell, who authored the *Lloyd* opinion, wrote one of the two concurring opinions. He argued that *Lloyd* did not overturn the *Logan Valley Plaza* decision of the Court and pointed out that the law had been unclear and uncertain since the 1968 opinion analogized the shopping center with the company town. (Both the Powell and the Stewart opinions made the same mistake, claiming that Marshall paired the shopping center with the company town. He did not do that: *Logan Valley Plaza* stated that the shopping center was the functional equivalent of the business district within the company town. To argue the contrary is erroneous, careless adjudication.) Justice Black had disagreed with that analogy. Powell, in *Hudgens*, now agreed "with Justice Black that the opinions in these cases—*Marsh*, *Logan Valley*, and *Lloyd*—cannot be harmonized in a principled way. Upon more mature thought I have concluded that we would have been wiser in *Lloyd* to have confronted this disharmony rather than draw distinctions based on rather attentuated factual differences. The Court's opinion, clarifying the law, is desirable."[80]

CONCURRING OPINION: MR. JUSTICE WHITE

Justice White also concurred. Unlike the other opinions already discussed, he did not think it was necessary to "inter Logan Valley Plaza"[81] nor did *Lloyd* in 1971 do it then. For White, the swing vote in the *Lloyd* five-man majority, that opinion did not overrule *Logan Valley* "and I would not, somewhat after the fact, say that it did." He believed that *Lloyd* was not holding in *Hudgens* "for it does not cover the facts of this case."[82] There was no need to admit error, as Powell and Burger had done, for no error existed. *Logan Valley* should have remained as precedent, wrote the justice who dissented in that decision of the Warren Court, for *Lloyd* had not overturned it directly or silently.

DISSENTING OPINION: MR. JUSTICE MARSHALL (JOINED BY MR. JUSTICE BRENNAN)

Justice Marshall forcefully objected to the death of the rationale of *Logan Valley Plaza*. He argued that the NLRB had decided *Hudgens* on statutory grounds and that the Court should have been bound by self-restraint rules of constitutional adjudication to limit its examination to the statutory questions raised by management in the case: whether the NLRB correctly followed the *Babcock and Wilcox* requirements. The Stewart opinion argued Marshall, "reached out, bypassing the statutory question, to overrule a constitutionally based decision." In so acting, the plurality opinion "surely departs from traditional modes of adjudication."[83]

Arguing that *Munn* v. *Illinois*, an 1877 case that spoke of businesses affected with the public interest submitting to controls "by the public for the common good," was precedent for placing constitutional control upon the private shopping center, Marshall continued to argue the validity of his 1968 opinion.[84] He was "unwilling to grant shopping center owners the commercial advantages obtained by assuming control of the public forum without correspondingly assuming its responsibilities."[85]

Conceding the precedential value of *Lloyd*, Marshall argued that *Logan Valley Plaza* could not be read as broadly as it had been by state courts in California, Washington, and New York. But *Lloyd* only narrowed *Logan Valley*; it did not overturn it. "I cannot understand the Court's bypassing a purely statutory question to overrule a First Amendment decision less than ten years old." *Logan Valley* "has been laid to rest without ever having been accorded a proper burial."[86]

Marshall spoke of the realities of the shopping center, once again for the third time (twice in dissenting opinions). He concluded his dissent by pointing out that Powell's 1971 opinion carefully preserved the fact situation holding in *Logan Valley* (that picketing related to shopping center functions could take place where there were not available alternatives for reaching the general public). "Upon reflection," confessed Marshall, "I am of the view that the two decisions are reconcilable."[87]

The Court in *Hudgens* attempted to rectify and clarify error and confusion created by earlier judicial decisions, NLRB judgments, and actions of state courts. The question that has to be answered now is whether the 1976 judgment of the Court was good overturn.

THE *HUDGENS* OVERTURN:
CRAFTSMANSHIP OR FIAT?

The *Hudgens* overturn was unlike the other two discussed in this book. It was not a majority opinion of the Court; it was, instead, a plurality opinion. Such "no clear majority" opinions generally have very little precedential value because the Court was fairly equally divided on the rationale question.[88] Additionally, it was a judgment of a Supreme Court that was, in the eyes of the legal profession and political commentators, of a different ideological persuasion and reflected the compositional changes in Supreme Court personnel since 1968. Justice Marshall noted this factor in 1971, in his *Lloyd* dissent: "I am aware that the composition of this Court has radically changed in four years."[89] A constitutional scholar noted for his conservative views wrote: "There is something disturbing about the proposition that a watershed in constitutional law is marked not by changes in the constitutional text, or by changes in social conditions, but is essentially the result of changes in personnel."[90]

The *Hudgens* plurality and concurring opinions also evidenced obvious partisan disdain for a decision of the Court that allegedly damaged property rights and fear of the consequences if *Logan Valley Plaza* was not overturned. Hudgens "spelled multilateral retrenchment on three fronts: 1) the public forum doctrine, 2) the concept of state action/function [which was dramatically narrowed in *Hudgens*], and 3) constitutional regard for labor picketing."[91] Such obvious hostility toward conventional doctrines, creatively expanded by earlier Court majorities, is not statesmanlike.

A basic question that was raised in these and all other overturn actions is whether the Constitution was faithfully adhered to by the majority, taking into account changed economic and social conditions in America. A statesmanlike overturn of an earlier judgment of the Court is one in which the Court expands creatively the ideal element of the society. *Hammer* v. *Dagenhart* and *Minersville* v. *Gobitis* were considered anachronisms because of the absence of creative expansion and the fears evidenced by majorities as to the consequences if they did not act in the way they did. *Lloyd* and *Hudgens* are two additional anachronisms, with this vital difference: they overturned an earlier judgment of the Court that was reasonable. *Lloyd* and *Hudgens* were examples not of judicial craftsmanship but of judicial fiat.

RIGHTNESS OF THE OPINION

Was *Logan Valley Plaza* an erroneous decision? Justice Stewart never engaged in any careful discussion and evaluation of the correctness of the 1968 decision of the Warren Court. Had he done so, it may very well have proved awkward for him, for he had voted with Justice Marshall in 1968 and 1971. When Justices Black, Douglas, and Murphy recanted in *Opelika*, it was an open admission of error—with a set of reasons presented for their change of mind. But Stewart presented no such justification for change of mind; his action was simply judicial fiat.

Logan Valley Plaza was not discussed meritoriously because to do so fairly would have been to validate that 1968 opinion with respect to the correctness of its view of shopping centers: "The court refuses to recognize the new role of the shopping center as the hub of economic and social activity in the suburban community."[92] The decisions were reached in *Lloyd* and in *Hudgens* without ever examining the weight of interests of the shopping center owner in excluding all expressive activities from his premises. Only Justice White was aware of this dilemma, and his concurring opinion argued for the retention of *Logan Valley* to allow some type of protest activity within the private shopping mall.

Hudgens returned to the narrow view of state action sanctioned in *Lloyd* and in *Marsh:* when private property assumes all the characteristics of the public municipality, and only then, it rises to the level of state function/action. The decision was a housecleaning operation but one that swept a reasonable, incremental expansion of a constitutional concept (in light of changing economic and social change) out the door. Instead of accepting the reality of economic expansion and social mobility, the Court majority, concerned about the continued sanctity of private property, rejected reality and "equated the shopping center owner's right to privacy to that of a private home owner."[93] If the property center/home is the owner's castle, then free expression can enter only at the discretion of the owner. The First Amendment by direct implication was dramatically neutered by the judgments of the majorities in *Lloyd* and *Hudgens*.

Logan Valley Plaza had creatively expanded the right of free expression, incrementally, in light of the reality of the shopping center. Law, Marshall was saying in that opinion, must change to meet social and economic changes or it will no longer be relevant. *Hudgens* returns the law to the 1945 judgment of the Court in *Marsh*. Stewart's opinion suggests that nothing has changed since the war ended in that year; that the majority of Americans still shop in small grocery stores and that everybody greets each other by first name in commercial and economic matters. This erroneous judgment overturned *Logan Valley Plaza*. If error existed, it was the error of the justices who refused to accept the modern reality and who feared that the owner's (in these cases, a large multifaceted corporation, not a single person) rights would be atrophied by the invasion of countless protesters onto his property. If there was carelessness and fiat, it was to be found in the overturn judgment of the Court.

DEFINITENESS OF THE OPINION

An overturn is justfied if there is a need for clarity in law because of changed conditions in society. *Logan Valley Plaza* took cognizance of changing economic and social conditions and began to develop the law in light of these realities. The lack of clarity developed when the Nixon Court in 1971, in a bewildering, illogical display of judicial fiat, wrote *Central Hardware* and *Lloyd*. In opinions that followed each other in the *United States Reporter, Logan Valley* was used in *Central* but rejected in *Lloyd*. Furthermore the *Lloyd* majority misconstrued the *Logan Valley* majority's analogy between the private town and the shopping center.

Hudgens accepted the "perversive reading of Logan Valley in Lloyd, thereby deceptively bootstrapping the former into a seemingly indefensible posture."[94]

If there was a lack of clarity in *Logan*, it was due to the majorities' fiats in 1971 and 1976. There were no errors in the *Logan Valley Plaza* decision with respect to the existence and reality of the modern shopping center. While *Logan Valley* could have been a purely labor-management case, in light of the NLRA, because there was no discussion of the powers of the NLRB in the lower courts, Marshall had no option but to hear the case on the constitutional arguments (but limiting the judgment of the Court to the facts of the labor dispute). The overturns were poor because they added to the uncertainty of the law.

THE PRINCIPLES

The question raised earlier was whether *Hudgens* or *Logan Valley Plaza* adapted the Constitution and its essential principles to modern economic and social changes. It is clear that the 1968 opinion overturned by *Hudgens* was consistent with the vision and the intent of the framers.

Hudgens is a retreat from earlier views that reflected and recognized that the spread of privately owned shopping centers demanded a reassessment of traditional views on the availability of private property for use as a forum for free expression.[95]

Hudgens, drawing the distinction between the downtown merchant who was subject to protest from consumers (labor) in front of his store because of his nearness to the public streets and the private shopping center corporation, which could exclude free expression from the malls and plazas, "ignored the traditional wisdom of the Constitution."[96] While private property rights are protected in the Constitution, the Constitution's very existence is predicated on the people's right to know and be informed. Without knowledge and the forum necessary for the communication of ideas, democracy perishes. To deny citizens, especially those who cannot afford to pay for television time, the right to a forum in areas where the public generally and peacefully congregates, is to deny democracy the necessary prerequisites for satisfactory performance. The right to know and to be informed is and has always been a hallmark of the American system of constitutional law. The *Hudgens* opinion, by denying free expression in the shopping center, ignores the vision of the Constitution makers. For that reason, *Hudgens* is poor overturn.

Blaustein and Field have discussed three criteria that constitute an "unwarranted overturn": little, if any, adequate consideration of the reasoning of the earlier decision, little, if any, weight given to the values inherent in that earlier opinion of the Court, and overruling "obviously" caused by changes in court personnel.[97] *Hudgens* meets all three criteria. There was no carefully done analysis of the correctness of Logan Valley. There was no credence given to the values inherent in Logan Valley, except for some comments by Justice White. There was the obvious change in personnel and in judicial philosophy, which was not visible in the other overturns discussed in this book, when the Warren Court expired and the Nixon Court emerged at the time of *Lloyd*.

The *Hudgens* judgment was an unwarranted overturn. It was sloppy and illogical, and it reflected a basic fear of change; it added to the law's uncertainty and negated the value of a basic constitutional principle—freedom of expression—in an area of social activity that has become the symbol of modern America—the shopping center. It did not rise to the level of a principled, statesmanlike, judicial decision. Fiat rather than craftsmanship took place when the Court decided both *Lloyd* and *Hudgens*.

SUMMARY

The *Hudgens* overturn of *Logan Valley Plaza* was a decision of the Supreme Court that exhibited all the attributes of a poor overturn. Coming on the heels of a dramatic change in Court personnel when President Nixon appointed four new members, the Nixon Court's decisions in *Central Hardware* and *Lloyd* were contradictory, unclear, and inexplicable unless Powell had an "extraordinary respect for stare decisis or the desire for its appearance."[98] By the time of *Hudgens* the respect for stare decisis with regard to this area had disappeared. *Logan Valley* was overturned because the Court majority's political and philosophical views regarded the 1968 opinion with disdain. It was disgarded without even a decent burial.

NOTES

1. See generally Thomas Thorson, *The Logic of Democracy* (New York: Norton, 1961). "Exercise of First Amendment Rights in Private Shopping Centers, *Washington University Law Review* (1973): 427.

2. *Hague* v. *CIO*, 307 U.S. 496 (1939).

3. See *Adderly* v. *Florida*, 385 U.S. 39 (1966).

4. See *Tinker* v. *DesMoines School Board* 393 U.S. 503 (1969) *United States* v. *O'Brien* 391 U.S. 367 (1968), and *Thornhill* v. *Alabama* 310 U.S. 88 (1940).

5. Evelyn Lambeth, "Hudgens—A Final Definition of the Public Forum?" *Wake Forest Law Review* 13 (Spring 1977): 140.

6. M. Russell Kruse, Jr., "From Logan Valley Plaza to Hyde Park and Back: Shopping Centers and Free Speech," *Southwestern Law Journal* 26 (November 1972): 571.

7. Robert Kochly, "The Shopping Center: Quasi Public Forum for Suburbia," *University of San Francisco Law Review* 6 (October 1971): 104.

8. *Marsh* v. *Alabama*, 326 U.S. 501 (1945), at 503.

9. Robin Dwyer, "Shopping Centers after Hudgens," *St. Mary's Law Journal* 8 (1976): 367.

10. *The Civil Rights Cases*, 1883, 109 U.S. 3.

11. Lambeth, op. cit., p. 141.

12. *Marsh*, at 506.

13. Ibid., at 509.

14. Ralph Boccarosse, "Freedom of Expression in Shopping Centers—A Reevaluation by the Burger Court," *Catholic University Law Review* 22 (Summer 1973): 811.

15. *Marsh*, at 510–511.

16. Ibid., at 512.

17. Ibid.

18. *Buck* v. *Bell*, 274 U.S. 200 (1927), at 208.

19. "The First Amendment and the Problem of Access to Migrant Labor Camps After Lloyd v. Tanner," *Cornell Law Review* 61 (April 1976): 561–564.

20. Lambeth, op. cit., p. 147.

21. *National Labor Relations Board* v. *Babcock and Wilcox Company*, 351 U.S. 105 (1956), at 106-107.

22. Ibid., at 112.

23. W. C. Owen, "Plazas, Parking Lots, and Picketing," *Labor Law Journal* 23 (December 1972): 743.

24. "Shopping Centers and Labor Relations Law," *Stanford Law Review* 10 (1958): 700.

25. Gerry Gibson, "Property Rights Triumphant in the Shopping Center," *University of Florida Law Review* 28 (April 1976): 1033.

26. *Amalgamated Food Employees Union 590* v. *Logan Valley Plaza*, 391 U.S. 308 (1968), at 317.

27. Gibson, op. cit., p. 1034.

28. Ibid., p. 319. See *Marsh*, at 502, 506.

29. Lambeth, op. cit., p. 143

30. Logan, at 319. n. 9.

31. Ibid., at 319-320.

32. Ibid., at 326.

33. Ibid., at 326-327.

34. Ibid., at 330.

35. Ibid., at 333-334.

36. Ibid., at 339.

37. Owen, "Plazas, Parking Lots, and Picketing," op. cit., p. 745.

38. Boccarosse, op. cit., p. 819.

39. Morris Forkosch, "Picketing in Shopping Centers," *Washington and Lee Law Review* 26 (December 1969): 252-253.

40. The subsequent paragraphs drew their information from: Morris, "Shopping Centers: Main Street Moves to the Mall," *Management Review* 58 (May 1969); Wenzlick, "Shopping Centers Still Gaining on Central Business District," *Real Estate Analyst* 34 (1970): 341; "Seeks Billions for New Centers," *Chain Store Age* (February 1971); Breckenfeld, "'Downtown' Has Fled to the Suburbs," *Fortune* 86 (October 1972); "Private Business Districts and the First Amendment," *Urban Law Annual* 7 (1974); "Growth of Shopping Centers in America," 105 *Sales Management* (November 1970); Weiss, "Expect 1000 Pedestrian Shopping Malls by 1980," *Advertising Age* 41 (September 1970); Young, "Shopping Centers: Downtown the Next Target," *Architectural Record* (October 1969); "Shopping Centers Grow into Shopping Cities," *Business Week*, September 4, 1971.

41. Stephen Felsenthal, "Free Speech on the Premises of Privately Owned Shopping Centers," *Wisconsin Law Review* (Fall, 1973): 619. "Consequently the shopping center should be seen as a public place just as traditional

municipal business districts have been."

42. See "Lloyd v. Tanner: The Demise of Logan Valley Plaza and the Disguise of Marsh," *Georgetown Law Journal* 61 (May 1973): 128; but cf. Vincent DeLuzio, "Shopping Centers and the Fourteenth Amendment: Public Function and State Need," *University of Pittsburgh Law Review* 33 (Fall 1971): 118. One source suggests that "it is now economically more efficient for cities to rely on private corporations to develop public business districts rather than for cities to fulfill this traditionally governmental function (due to lack of funds, etc.)" in "Lloyd v. Tanner: A Shopping Center Open for Business But Not for Dissent," *Maine Law Review* 25 (1973): 145.

43. Forkosch, op. cit., pp. 252–253.

44. Jesse Etelson, "Picketing and Freedom of Speech: Comes the Evolution," *John Marshall Journal of Practice and Procedure* 10 (Fall 1976): 18.

45. Boccarosse, op. cit., and DeLuzio, op. cit., passim.

46. *Central Hardware* v. *NLRB*, 407 U.S. 539 (1971), at 543–544.

47. Ibid., at 546–547.

48. Ibid., at 547.

49. Ibid., at 548.

50. Quoted in Boccarosse, op. cit., p. 810.

51. Quoted in "Lloyd v. Tanner: Shopping Center Open," p. 133.

52. *Lloyd Corporation* v. *Tanner*, 407 U.S. 551 (1971), at 562.

53. Ibid., at 568.

54. Ibid., at 568–569.

55. Ibid.

56. Ibid., at 576.

57. Ibid., at 583.

58. Ibid., at 580–581.

59. Barry Wilford, "Labor Picketing on Private Property and the Vexation of Logan Valley Plaza: The Nixon Court Responds in Hudgens," *Capital University Law Review* 6 (1976): at 261.

60. "Free Speech in the Marketplace," *University of Colorado Law Review* 44 (December 1972): 264.

61. Robert Lewis, "Free Speech and Property Rights Reequated: The Supreme Court Ascends from Logan Valley," *Labor Law Journal* 24 (April, 1973): 200.

62. Lambeth, op. cit., p. 144.

63. "Lloyd v. Tanner: Demise of Logan Valley Plaze," p. 1216.

64. "Free Speech in the Marketplace," p. 270.

65. "Shopping Centers," p. 710.

66. "Free Speech in the Marketplace," p. 263.

67. *Lloyd*, at 584.

68. Ibid.

69. Lambeth, op. cit., p. 150.

70. Ibid.

71. *Scott Hudgens* v. *NLRB,* 96 *S.Ct.*Reporter 1029 (1975), at 1033.

72. Ibid.

73. Ibid., at 1036.

74. Ibid., at 1035-1036.

75. Ibid., at 1036.

76. Ibid., at 1036-1037.

77. Ibid., at 1037.

78. Lambeth, op. cit., p. 152.

79. *Hudgens,* at 1037.

80. Ibid., at 1038-1039.

81. Ibid., at 1039.

82. Ibid.

83. Ibid., at 1040.

84. *Munn* v. *Illinois,* 94 U.S. 113 (1877).

85. Lambeth, op. cit., p. 156.

86. *Hudgens,* at 1044.

87. Ibid.

88. "No Clear Majority," *University of Chicago Law Review* 24 (1956): 101.

89. *Lloyd,* at 584.

90. Phillip Kurland, "1970 Term: Notes on the Emergence of the Burger Court," *The Supreme Court Review, 1971* (Chicago: University of Chicago Press, 1971), p. 265.

91. Wilford, op. cit., p. 273.

92. Gibson, op. cit., p. 1042.

93. *Ibid.,* p. 1043.

94. Wilford, op. cit., p. 263-264.

95. Gibson, op. cit., p. 1043.

96. *Dwyer,* op. cit., p. 373.

97. Albert Blaustein and Andrew Field, " 'Overruling' Opinions in the Supreme Court," *Michigan Law Review* 57 (December 1958): 175-176.

98. Comment, *"Lloyd* v. *Tanner;* The Demise of Logan Valley and the Disguise of Marsh," op. cit., at 1219.

6 The Importance of Judicial Craftsmanship

THE DYNAMICS OF THE CONSTITUTION

The Constitution makers were concerned about the maintenance of the union of states. The Constitution's implied premises—social compact, popular sovereignty, governments limited in powers—spelled out a gamble that the framers took with the people and with themselves. Under great stress, they created a blueprint of government in the hopes of fostering a "more perfect Union." With a combination of political compromise and genius, in making the document for the nation they used broad brush strokes.

"Clarity does not obtain" in the Constitution, wrote a constitutional scholar. It is framed in generalities, "broad principles stated illumined slightly."[1] The fact that the political compromise, that general blueprint of government, becomes the higher law for the society, is due in large part to the courts. The judiciary in America has transformed the document into a higher law, "a Common Law,"[2] and accounts for the dynamism of the Constitution—and for its reverence and its vitality.

THE SUPREME COURT AND THE CONSTITUTION

CONSTITUTIONAL ADJUDICATION

Article III of the Constitution states that "judicial power of the United States Supreme Court extends to all cases, in law and equity, arising under this Constitution." The Constitution's continuing strength, flexibility, and vitality stem from the fact that the Supreme Court, since its inception, has felt compelled—by virtue of the justices' oath to see that justice is done—to give meaning to the general phrases of the Constitution. Given the presence of a legitimate case or controversy (the conflict is properly before the Court), the justices of the Supreme Court have, in the words of Marshall, "expounded" upon the meaning of the general terms in "response to life and experience."³ "Litigation is the vehicle by which the fundamental principles rooted in our Constitution are given content and relevance in each generation. In short, constitutional adjudication is the genius of our democracy and its noblest attribute."⁴

This judicial reinterpretation of the words of the Constitution is, optimally, a process of adjudication whereby the "judge draws his inspiration from its consecrated principles."⁵ This process of examining the meaning of the constitutional concepts is the highest, and most difficult, form of judicial labor. In America the courts are used to resolve major questions of political power and personal liberties; litigants come to the Supreme Court on appeal from the lower courts challenging the way in which legislation is passed by Congress. The law exists to resolve such disputes and the courts, especially the Supreme Court, must deal with these important legal and political constitutional questions.

Federal Courts, including the Supreme Court, do not pass on constitutional questions because there is a special function vested in them to enforce the Constitution or police the other agencies of government. They do so rather for the reason that they must decide a litigated issue that is otherwise within their jurisdiction and in doing so must give effect to the supreme law of the land.⁶

In dealing with these constitutional questions, the Court inevitably takes upon itself the role of supreme arbiter, legitimator, interpreter, and educator of and for the governmental process. This occurs when the Court employs judicial review to examine these problems.

JUDICIAL REVIEW

Judicial review is the power of a court to declare an action of a political actor, either state or national, in conflict with the Constitution and therefore null and void. Since *Marbury* v. *Madison* (1803), the power of the Supreme Court to so act has been challenged, but it has been accepted as one of the necessities of the governmental process.[7] The judiciary, said James Madison, "is truly the only defensive armor of the federal government, or rather, for the Constitution. Strip it of that armor and the door is wide open for nullification, anarchy, and convulsion."[8] Using its power to declare an action of Congress, or the president, or a state legislature unconstitutional, the Court has given meaning to those slightly illuminated principles in the Constitution. Since *Marbury*, over 900 state actions and 120 federal actions have been declared unconstitutional by the Supreme Court.

Judicial review, then, is the process through which the fundamental law retains its vitality and through which citizens have been able to raise questions concerning the limits of governmental power that in another society would be resolved through force of arms. The Supreme Court has become, through the judicious use of this power, the ultimate arbiter of the American constitutional system.

THE PRINCIPLED OPINION OF THE SUPREME COURT

In employing judicial review, justices interpret anew the "consecrated principles," of the Constitution. In the process of constitutional adjudication, there are standards of criteria, "moral limits," that the justices are obligated to follow if the opinion is to be considered a principled, craftsmanlike product.[9] Judges cannot decide cases solely on the basis of personal preference or bias. In drawing upon their life experiences, they must balance their personal views with the views of society when "interpreting the open ended concepts of the Constitution."[10] Judges' perceptions of goals for society are tempered by their understanding of the taught tradition of the law.

These taught traditions emphasize judicial integrity, importance of precedent and stare decisis, importance of procedural guidelines, presumption of legislative validity, and consciousness of societal consensus on issues. Judges have roles imposed upon them "both personally and institutionally, i.e., that of serving as a filter for the values of society. The living force of others' values causes a judge to implement something other than his own individual biases and sympathies."[11]

Balancing these various elements—weighing history and the meanings of concepts, considering the normal claims of continuity, and taking into account the changes that have taken place in life and law—the Court comes to a decision in a constitutional case.[12]

Decisions are considered principled and craftsmanlike because of the critical process of reasoning that leads to the judgment. A principled opinion is one in which the Court carefully evaluates the forces of change and the forces for continuity and, after such careful analysis and reflection on these constitutional issues, announces its judgment. The ultimate rightness of the judgment is impossible to estimate because of the incessant demands of life that call for reevaluation of even the most sacred of beliefs. What is of critical importance in the principled opinion is that the judgment has been reached, and explicated, in a manner that reflects the integrity and fairness of the Court.[13] If the Court has erred in its evaluation of facts, its view of the meaning of a concept, and so forth, the judicial error can be rectified in a number of ways.

Judicial fiat occurs when the Court, out of fear and concern that springs from the souls of well-intentioned justices, responds in a manner that suggests ad hoc rather than reasoned judgment. A Court majority that presents a judgment that does not answer questions raised in litigation or that answers questions not raised in the briefs or oral arguments, or that presents illogicial conclusions, or conclusions without presenting justifications for these conclusions or appears to use "a sliding scale of values, creates too great a risk of [appearing to be] ad hoc, unprincipled judicial intervention."[14]

The distinctive element that separates the principled opinion from judicial fiat is the "appeal to reason" that the former offers that the judicial decree lacks.[15] Both can, in the end, be wrong and both can later be changed through modification or discarding of precedent by another Court majority. But the judicial decree, or judicial fiat, damages the image and integrity of the judicial branch because of its nonjudicious characteristics. The Court is fallible, but it is the final court of justice in America and its judgments ought to be just and equitable; "judges must attend to *all considerations relevant* to just and equitable decisions."[16]

There are no short cuts that can be taken in the process of creating the principled decision; attending to all considerations relevant to a just decision is a burden to carry. But this is precisely what distinguishes the judiciary in America from the other branches of government.

Unlike legislators and the presidents, the justices must justify their judgments in open court and before the bar of justice. Not to do so or to do a poor job of explaining the reasons for a judgment makes the Court no less and no more a legislator than the Congress. While it is true that "the greatest tides and currents which engulf the rest of men, do not turn aside in their course and pass the judges idly by." these jurists must respond to crises in a manner different from that of legislative or executive response.[17]

The judges' function (recall Madison's view) is the only defensive armor the Constitution has in the face of intentional or unintentional abuse of its concepts, powers, obligations, and responsibilities by other governmental actors. If the judiciary acts in an unprincipled manner, who controls the custodians? Who, in that eventuality, will assume the mantle of final arbiter of constitutional crisis?

Symbols are important, as Frankfurter suggested in the flag salute cases, and the symbol of the Court as a fair and just tribunal where constitutional arguments will be made and carefully evaluated by the justices is a symbol of fundamental societal importance. Acting in a principled way reflects upon the integrity of the Court and reinforces the positive image of the courts in America. Constant judicial fiat damages the Court's reputation and has the potential for far more serious dislocations in the society. If the Court is seen as a partisan political actor, acting in an ad hoc, nonprincipled manner in deciding cases before it, then the law as a process for resolving controversy fairly and equitably no longer has relevancy.

JUDICIAL OVERTURN OF
CONSTITUTIONAL DECISIONS

A dramatic part of this process of constitutional adjudication has been direct overturn of Supreme Court opinions thought by a later Court majority to have been improperly decided. Decision making by judges is an action of fallible men. Errors of judgment will be made—errors in reasoning, in interpreting facts, and in projecting future events and possibilities. In the process of constitutional adjudication, the justices must never lose sight of the dynamic nature of the Constitution; their function is to expound upon the document and not automatically apply what earlier jurists have said about that document. Overturn is thus a choice available to the Court. It becomes a viable option when, for a number of reasons, the earlier precedent no longer seems to be appropriate or correct.

WHY DOES THE SUPREME COURT
OVERTURN PRECEDENT?

The three basic, although not the necessary and sufficient conditions for overturn, justifications that the Court has given for overturning earlier Court precedent have been rightness (earlier error realized); definiteness (lack of clarity in the law because of changed conditions, later judgments, and so forth), and principleness (the earlier opinion did not evaluate in a principled manner the history of the concept, intentions of the framers, or the vision of the men who authored the concepts).

Whether confronted by earlier principled judgments whose reasoning has fallen into disrepute because of changes in life and law (such as the Frankfurter opinion in *Gobitis*) or confronted by earlier judicial fiat (the *Hammer* majority opinion of Day). a Court majority, faced with the option of following these erroneous precedents or overturning them, has overturned. The Court in this regard "has always been to some extent a self-correcting agency."[18]

The underlying reason for direct overturn is that the Constitution is constantly being reinterpreted by the Court in various cases and controversies and, although stare decisis is the normal policy, the Supreme Court is not bound to precedent when the Constitution's meaning and intent is made part of the litigation. In light of its oath to uphold the Constitution, an opinion of the Supreme Court "is always open to discussion when it is supposed to have been found in error," wrote Chief Justice Taney.[19] Error, whether factual, legal, personal (the prejudices and fears of judges), normative, intentional or unintentional, occasionally leads to direct overturn. The question raised in this book has been whether, in the process of direct overturn, the Court majority has done a statesman-like job.

THE QUALITIES OF A GOOD OVERTURN

A good overturn opinion contains the characteristics of a principled opinion. Overturning an earlier precedent is no easy matter, and great care has to be taken in assuring the audience of legal scholars, lower court judges, and the public at large that the judgment to overturn was not a hasty, ad hoc decision. The weighing process, if anything, has to be more precise; the balancing of the importance of maintaining earlier precedent versus the costs of retaining it in light of changes in the society must be done in a reasoned, measured way by the Court majority.

In addition to the ordinary burden that the forces of reason place on justices when they decide a case, the additional burden is to decide the case in light of the Constitution while at the same time carefully, rationally overturning an earlier opinion of the Court that, if applied, would have forced the Court to respond to the case or controversy in a different way. As Blaustein and Field stated, judicial overturn is judicial activity of the very highest labor.

The principled judicial overturn, in effect, treats the overturned opinion as a premature formulation of an earlier Court's perception of a constitutional concept. By implication, the principled overturn opinion also suggests that it too may very well prove to be premature. The principled opinion accepts the evolutionary nature of the law. The constitutional concepts are reinterpreted in the light of changes that have taken place since the earlier opinion was written. This is the reality of constitutional adjudication. But if social forces produce legal actions, so do the justices' views of these normative concepts. In short, the principled overturn decision is goal oriented. The illumination of the interstices of the Constitution is the goal of justices when they hear cases that deal with its meaning. If their responsibility is to the words of the Constitution, then the Court must overturn an earlier opinion that seems to be erroneous.

The earlier opinion must be seen to have been erroneous before it is overturned. Reasons have to be presented for the overturn. A weighty examination of the merits inherent in keeping the precedent as opposed to the merits of overturn must take place and be visible to the various Court publics. Poor overturns (such as the *Hudgens* overturn of *Logan Valley Plaza*) exhibit divisiveness, lack of good reasons, lack of weighty discussion of the merits and demerits of the earlier decision, and no examination of the consequences of overturning the earlier opinion. In short, the poor overturn is the unprincipled decision or the unwarranted overturn.

The unwarranted overturn suggests that the overturn Court majority did not weigh the merits of the earlier opinion carefully, was ideologically motivated, and ignored the inherent value with respect to its interpretation of enduring constitutional concepts. The *Hudgens* majority/plurality judgment smacked of ad hoc, personal, decision making by a small group of self-appointed guardians of private property. The reputation of the Court suffers when it acts in that manner; the law suffers when its highest court turns the adjudicatory process into an ideological campaign. When the Court becomes an obviously result-oriented tribunal, justice suffers.

THE IMPORTANCE OF
JUDICIAL CRAFTSMANSHIP

"The strength of our common law is that it can reconcile contradictions," wrote Jan Deutsch.[20] Constitutional law, given the reality of judicial review and overturn of precedents that have been shown to have been erroneous, has become the "common law in the hands of the judges, developed by common law process and in the common law tradition."[21] The Constitution, given the antinomy between continuity and change, has been since *Marbury* v. *Madison* an "open Constitution."[22] Its open-endedness is a reflection of fallible humanity.

Confronted with conflicting demands calling for change and stability, the Supreme Court must in good faith reconcile these contradictory values. In a dialectical fashion and in a principled judgment, it must overcome the contradictions by evolving new law in line with the enduring principles of the Constitution. And, at some time in the future, that principled overturn decision may, in turn, be modified, distinguished, discarded, or ignored.[23]

Anything less than an honest, sincere attempt to arrive at the just decision by following the criteria for a principled decision enumerated above, regardless of the durability of that decision in subsequent generations of litigation, damages the fabric of the society. That fabric is the conception of law as an equitable resolver of controversy in a democratic civilization. "Law," wrote Justice Holmes, "is a statement of the circumstances in which public force will be brought to bear upon men through the courts."[24] If those circumstances are clouded because the courts are thought to be partisan participants on behalf of certain causes espoused by dominant social forces, then the ability of the society to resolve its conflicts pacifically is jeopardized. If law is to be a reconciling process, then judges have to act in a statesmanslike manner. They must follow the taught traditions of the law, drawing upon life experiences, and ever balancing the inherent contradictions that beset the human condition. When announcing their reasoned judgment they must do so in a craftsmanlike opinion. We must expect no less of the Supreme Court justices; we can demand no more than that.

NOTES

1. Herbert Wechsler, *The Courts and the Constitution,* The John A. Sibley Lectures in Law (Athens: University of Georgia, 1965), p. 14.

2. Louis Henkin, "Constitutional Fathers—Constitutional Sons," *Minnesota Law Review* 60 (June 1976): 1130.

3. Ibid., 1140.

4. Tom C. Clark, "Introduction: Civil Liberties," *Hastings Constitutional Law Quarterly* 1 (1974): 1.

5. Benjamin Cardozo, *The Nature of the Judicial Process* (New Haven: Yale University Press, 1921): p. 97.

6. Wechsler, op. cit., p. 7.

7. Attorney General Biddle, quoted in Henry J. Abraham, *The Judiciary: The Supreme Court in the Judiciary Process* (Boston: Allyn and Bacon, 1977), p. 169.

8. Charles Warren, *The Supreme Court in the United States History* (Boston: Little, Brown, 1937), 1:740.

9. Wechsler, op. cit., p. 12.

10. Ibid., at 14.

11. Jan Deutsch, *Jurisprudence,* op. cit., p. 880.

12. Wechsler, op. cit., p. 15.

13. "The real benefit of judicial review is that it is a process of constitutional adjudication that is concerned with principle. The Court must give reasons for what it does; reasons that appeal to the intellect and the ethical sense of the country. The Court introduces a moral element into our political life." Anthony Lewis, "A Constitutional Faith," *Hastings Constitutional Law Quarterly* 3 (Summer 1976): 686.

14. Henry Abraham, "Of Myths, Motives, Motivations, and Morality: Some Observations on the Burger Court's Record on Civil Rights and Liberties," *Notre Dame Lawyer* 52 (October 1976): 86.

15. Wechsler, p. 15.

16. Blackstone, *Legal Reasoning,* op. cit., p. 322.

17. Cardozo, op. cit., p. 168.

18. Wechsler, op. cit., p. 4.

19. Quoted in ibid.

20. Deutsch, op. cit., p. 881.

21. Henkin, op. cit., p. 1130.

22. Ibid., p. 1135.

23. Deutsch, op. cit., p. 881.

24. *American Banana Company* v. *United Fruit Company,* 213 U.S. 347 (1908), at 356.

Bibliography

BOOKS

Abraham, Henry J. *Courts and Judges*. New York: Oxford University Press, 1959.

———. *The Judicial Process*. New York: Oxford University Press, 1975.

———. *The Judiciary: The Supreme Court in the Governmental Process*, 4th ed. Boston: Allyn and Bacon, 1977.

Andrews, William G. *Constitutions and Constitutionalism*. New York: Van Nostrand, 1961.

Ball, Howard. *The Warren Court's Perceptions of Democracy*. Rutherford, N.J.: Fairleigh Dickinson University Press, 1972.

———. *No Pledge of Privacy*. New York: Kennikat Press, 1977.

Bickel, Alexander. *The Least Dangerous Branch*. Indianapolis: Bobbs-Merrill, 1962.

Black, Charles L. Jr. *The People and the Court*. New York: Macmillan, 1960.

Bodenheimer, Edward. *Jurisprudence*. New York: McGraw Hill, 1947.

Braden, George D. *The Search for Objectivity in Constitutional Law*. New Haven: Yale University Press. 1948.

Cahn, Edmond. *The Sense of Injustice*. New York: New York University Press. 1951.

———. *The Moral Decision*. Indiana University Press, 1959.

Cardozo, Benjamin, *The Nature of the Judicial Process*. New Haven: Yale University Press, 1921.

———. *The Growth of the Law*. New Haven: Yale University Press. 1924.

———. *The Paradoxes of Legal Science*. New York: Columbia University Press, 1928.

Carr, Robert C. *Democracy and the Supreme Court*. Norman: University of Oklahoma Press, 1936.

Corwin, Edward S. *The Doctrine of Judicial Review*. Princeton: Princeton University Press, 1914.

———. *The Commerce Power versus States Rights*. Princeton: Princeton University Press. 1936.

———. *Total War and the Constitution*. New York: A.A. Knopf, 1947.

Cowan, Theodore. *The American Jurisprudence Reader*. New York: Oceana, 1955.

Crosskey, William W. *Politics and the Constitution in the History of the United States*. Chicago: University of Chicago Press. 1953.

Douglas, William O. *We the Judges*. New York: Doubleday. 1949.

Farrand, Max, ed. *The Records of the Federal Constitutional Convention of 1787*. New Haven: Yale University Press, 1911.

Frank, Jerome F. *Law and the Modern Mind*. New York: Brentano. 1949.

Frankfurter, Felix. *The Commerce Clause under Marshall, Taney, and Waite*. Durham: University of North Carolina Press. 1937.

———. *Of Law and Men*. New York: Harcourt, Brace. 1956.

Freund, Paul A. *The Supreme Court of the United States*. New York: Meridian Books. 1961.

Goldberg, Arthur J. *Equal Justice: The Warren Court Era of the Supreme Court*. New York: Farrar, Straus, and Giroux, 1971.

Hart, H. L. A. *The Concept of Law*. London: Clarendon Press, 1961.

Jackson, Robert H. *The Struggle for Judicial Supremacy*. New York: Alfred A. Knopf, 1941.

———. *The Supreme Court in the American System of Government*. Boston: Harvard University Press. 1955.

Levi, Edward. *Introduction to Legal Reasoning*. Chicago: University of Chicago Press, 1960.

Levy, Beryl. *Our Constitution: Tool or Testament*. New York: Kennikat, 1941.

Levy, Leonard. *The Supreme Court under Earl Warren*. New York: Quadrangle Books, 1972.

Lockhard, Duane. *The American Constitution*. St. Paul: West Publishing. 1975.

Llewellyn, Karl N. *The Bramble Bush*. New York: Oceana. 1957.

———. *The Common Law Tradition*. New York: Little, Brown. 1960.

———. *Essays in Jurisprudence*. Chicago: University of Chicago Press. 1962.

Mason, Arthur T. *Harlan Fiske Stone: Pillar of the Law*. New York: Viking Press, 1956.

Mendelson, Wallace. *Capitalism, Democracy and the Supreme Court*.

New York: Appelton-Century-Crofts. 1960.

Murphy, William and Pritchett, Charles H. ed. *Courts, Judges, and Politics.* New York: Random House. 1975.

Paton, George W. *A Textbook of Jurisprudence.* London: Oxford at the Clarendon Press, 1961

Pound, Roscoe. *The Spirit of the Common Law.* Marshall Jones, 1931.

―――. *The Future of the Common Law.* Boston: Harvard University Press. 1937.

―――. *Social Control Through Law.* New Haven: Yale University Press. 1942.

―――. *Law Finding Through Experience and Reason.* Athens: Georgia Press. 1960.

Roberts, Owen J. *The Court and the Constitution.* Boston: Harvard University Press, 1951.

Rodell, Fred. *Nine Men.* New York: Random House, 1955.

Rosenblum, Victor G. *Law as a Political Instrument.* New York: Doubleday. 1965.

Schmidhauser, John R. *The Supreme Court.* New York: Holt. 1960.

Swisher, Carl B. *American Constitutional Development.* Boston: Little, Brown. 1954.

Thorson, Thomas. *The Logic of Democracy.* New York: Norton and Company, 1961.

Warren, Charles. *The Supreme Court in the United States History.* Boston: Little, Brown, 1937.

―――. *The Making of the Constitution.* Boston: Little, Brown. 1937.

Wasserstrom, Richard A. *The Judicial Decision.* Palo Alto: Stanford University Press. 1961.

White, Theodore. *Breach of Faith.* New York: Atheneum, 1975.

Wright, Benjamin. *The Contract Clause of the Constitution.* Boston: Harvard University Press. 1938.

ARTICLES

Abraham, Henry. "Of Myths, Motives, Motivations, and Morality: Some Observations on the Burger Court's Record on Civil Rights and Liberties." *Notre Dame Lawyer* 52 (October 1976).

Bernhardt, Charlotte. "Supreme Court Reversals on Constitutional Issues." *Cornell Law Quarterly* 34 (1948).

Boccarosse, Ralph. "Freedom of Expression in Shopping Centers―A Reevaluation by the Burger Court." *Catholic University Law Review,* 22, Summer 1973.

Bickle, Henry W. "The Commerce Power and Hammer v. Dagenhart." *University of Pennsylvania Law Review* 67 (1919).

Blaustein, Albert and Andrew Field. "'Overruling' Opinions in the Supreme Court." *Michigan Law Review* 57 (December 1958).

Brown, Wendell. "Construing the Constitution: A Trial Laywer's Plea for Stare Decisis." *American Bar Association Journal* 44 (August 1958).

Bruce, Andrew. "Interstate Commerce and Child Labor." *Minnesota Law Review* 3 (1918).

Carpenter, Charles. "Religious Freedom." *Southern California Law Review* 14 (1940).

Catlett, Fred. "The Development of the Doctrine of Stare Decisis and the Extent to Which it Should Be Applied." *Washington Law Review* 21 (1946).

Clark, Tom C. "Introduction: Civil Liberties." *Hastings Constitutional Law Quarterly* 1 (1974).

"Comment Supreme Court 'No Clear Majority' Decisions: A Study in Stare Decisis." *University of Chicago Law Review* 24 (Autumn 1956).

Corwin, Edward S. "Congress's power to prohibit Commerce: A Crucial Constitutional Issue." *Cornell Law Quarterly,* 18, June 1933.

Craven, J. Braxton. "Paean to Pragmatism." *North Carolina Law Review* 50 (1971).

Curries, David. "The Supreme Court and Federal Jurisdiction: 1975 Term." *The Supreme Court Review, 1976.* University of Chicago Press, 1977.

Deutsch, Jan G. "Jurisprudence of Affirmative Action: A Post Realist Analysis." *Georgetown Law Journal* 65 (April 1977).

———. "Neutrality, Legitimacy, and the Supreme Court: Some Intersections between Law and Political Science." *Stanford Law Review* 20 (1968).

Douglas, William O. "Stare Decisis." *Columbia Law Review* 49 (June 1949).

———. "The Task of Maintaining Our Liberties." *American Bar Association Journal,* 39, November 1953.

Dittfurth, David. "Judicial Reasoning and Social Change." *Indiana Law Journal* 50 (Winter 1975).

Dwyer, Robin. "Shopping Centers After Hudgens." *St. Mary's Law Journal* 8 (1976).

Etelson, Jesse. "Picketing and Freedom of Speech: Comes the Evolution." *John Marshall Journal of Practice and Procedure* 10 (Fall 1976).

Felsenthal, Stephen. "Free Speech on the Premises of Privately Owned Shopping Centers." *Wisconsin Law Review* (Fall 1973).

Forkosch, Morris. "Picketing in Shopping Centers." *Washington and Lee Law Review* 26 (December 1969).

Frankel, Lionel. "Humanist Law: The Need for Change in Legal Education —or—If Judges Do Not Find the Law, but Make It, What Do They Make It From?" *Utah Law Review,* no. 1 (January 1976).

Freedman, Samuel. "Continuity and Change: A Task of Reconciliation." *University of British Columbia Law Review* 8 (September 1973).

Gibson, Gerry. "Property Rights Triumphant in the Shopping Center." *University of Florida Law Review* 28 (April 1976).

Gilmore, Grant. "Legal Realism: Its Causes and Its Cure." *Yale Law Journal* 70 (June 1961).

Grant, J. A. C. "Commerce, Production, and the Fiscal Powers of Congress." *Yale Law Journal* 45 (March 1936).

Heller, Francis. "A Turning Point for Religious Liberty." *Virginia Law Review* 29 (September 1943).

Henkin, Louis. "Constitutional Fathers—Constitutional Sons." *Minnesota Law Review* 60 (June 1976).

Israel, Gerold. "Gideon v. Wainright: The 'Art' of Overruling," in P. Kurland, ed., *The Supreme Court Review, 1963.* Chicago: University of Chicago Press, 1963.

Jackson, Robert H. "Decisional Law and Stare Decisis." *American Bar Association Journal* 30 (March 1944).

Jacobsohn, Gary. "Constitutional Adjudication and Judicial Statesmanship." *Emory Law Journal* 23 (Winter 1974).

Kochly, Robert. "The Shopping Center: Quasi Public Forum for Suburbia." *University of San Francisco Law Review* 6 (October 1971).

Kruse, M. Russell, Jr. "From Logan Valley Plaza to Hyde Park and Back: Shopping Centers and Free Speech." *Southwestern Law Journal* 26 (November 1972).

Kurland, Phillip. "1970 Term: Notes on the Emergence of the Burger Court. *"The Supreme Court Review, 1971.* Chicago: University of Chicago Press, 1971.

Lambeth, Evelyn. "Hudgens—A Final Definition of the Public Forum?" *Wake Forest Law Review* 13 (Spring 1977).

Lewis, Robert. "Free Speech and Property Rights Reequated: The Supreme Court Ascends from Logan Valley." *Labor Law Journal* 24 (April 1973).

Lobingier, C. Sumner. "Precedent in Past and Present Legal Systems." *Michigan Law Review* 44 (September 1946).

Mendelson, Wallace. "Law and the Development of Nations." *Journal of Politics* 32 (May 1970).

Miller, Arthur S. "Notes on the Concept of the 'Living' Constitution." *George Washington Law Review* 31 (June 1963).

———. and D. S. Sastri. "Secrecy and the Supreme Court." *Buffalo Law Review* 22 (Spring 1973).

Noland, Jon D. "Stare Decisis and the Overruling of Constitutional Decisions in the Warren Years." *Valparaiso Law Review* 4 (June 1970).

Note. "Religious Freedom and Compulsory Saluting of the Flag." *University of Cincinnati Law Review.* 14, May 1940.

———. "Shopping Centers and Labor Relations Law." *Stanford Law Review.* 10, December 1958.

———. "Free Speech in the Marketplace." *University of Colorado Law Review.* 44, December 1972.

———. "Compulsory Flag Salute." *New York University Law Review.* 18 June 1940.

———. "Interstate Commerce and Darby" *Loyola Law Review.* 1, September 1941.

———. "Constitutionality of the Fair Labor Standards Act." *Illinois Law Review.* 35, May 1941.

———. "Lower Court Disavowal of Supreme Court Precedent." *Virginia Law Review.* 60, September 1974.

———. "Interstate Commerce and National Powers." *Missouri Law Review.* 6, Spring 1941.

———. "The First Amendment and the Problem of Access to Migrant Labor Camps After Lloyd v. Tanner." *Cornell Law Review.* 61, April 1976.

Owen, W. C. "Plazas, Parking Lots, and Picketing." *Labor Law Journal* 23 (December 1972).

Pound, Roscoe. "The Status of the Rule of Judicial Precedent." *University of Cincinnati Law Review* 14 (March 1940).

Powell, Thomas R. "The Child Labor Law, the Tenth Amendment, and the Commerce Clause." *Southern Law Quarterly* 3 (August 1918).

———. "Child Labor, Congress, and the Constitution." *North Carolina Law Review* 1 (November 1922).

Reed, Stanley. "Stare Decisis and Constitutional Law." *Pennsylvania Bar Association Quarterly* 33 (October 1937).

Remmlein, Madaleine, "Constitutional Implications of Compulsory Flag Salute Statutes." *George Washington Law Review.* 12, October 1943.

Schmidhauser, John R. "Stare Decisis, Dissent, and the Background of the Justices of the Supreme Court of the United States." *University of Toronto Law Journal* 14 (September 1962).

Shapiro, Martin. "Toward a Theory of Stare Decisis." *Journal of Legal Studies* 1 (January 1972).

Stern, Robert L. "The Commerce Clause and the National Economy." *Harvard Law Review* 59 (May–July 1946).

Tinsley, Mansur. "Legal Considerations Behind Statutes requiring a Salute to the Flag." *Rocky Mountain Law Review* 12 (Spring 1940).

Toomey, Alta. "Compulsory Flag Salutes and Religious Liberty." *University of Detroit Law Review* 4 (Fall 1940).

Waite, Edward F. "The Debt of Constitutional Law to Jehovah's Witnesses." *Minnesota Law Review* 28 (March 1944).

Warren, Earl. "The Law and the Future." *Fortune* 52 (November 1955).

Wechsler, Herbert. "Foreword: Toward Neutral Principles in Constitutional Adjudication." *Harvard Law Review* 73 (September 1961).

———. "The Courts and the Constitution." *The John A. Sibley Lectures in Law*, University of Georgia, Fall 1965.

Wilford, Barry. "Labor Picketing on Private Property and the Vexation of Logan Valley Plaza: The Nixon Court Responds in Hudgens." *Capital University Law Review* 6 (Spring 1976).

Wise, E. M. "The Doctrine of Stare Decisis." *Wayne State Law Review* 21 (July 1975).

Index

ABOUT THE AUTHOR

HOWARD BALL is Professor of Political Science at Mississippi State University. His earlier books include *Changing Perspectives in Contemporary Political Analysis, The Warren Court's Conceptions of Democracy,* and *No Pledge of Privacy: The Watergate Tapes Litigation, 1973-1974.*